OTHER TITLES IN THE SERIES

RAKU

John Mathieson

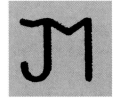

A & C Black · London

American Ceramic Society · Ohio

First published in Great Britain 2002
A & C Black Publishers Limited
37 Soho Square
London W1D 3QZ
www.acblack.com

ISBN 0-7136-5783-9

Published simultaneously in the USA by
The American Ceramic Society
735 Ceramic Place
Westerville, Ohio 43081, USA
www.ceramics.org

ISBN 1-57498-166-8

Cover illustrations

Front Rob Sollis, pot in fire.

Back John Mathieson, 'Vases for a Single Memory',
height (tallest): 25 cm (10 in.).

Frontispiece Pot by John Mathieson.

Book design: Alan Hamp
Cover design: Dorothy Moir

A & C Black uses paper produced with elemental
chlorine-free pulp, harvested from managed
sustainable forests.

Printed and bound in Singapore by Tien Wah Press.

Every effort has been made to ensure that all
of the information in this book is accurate.
Due to differing conditions, tools, materials,
and individual skills, the publisher cannot be
responsible for any injuries, losses, and other
damages that may result from the use of the
information in this book.

Contents

For Esmé, Mark and Sarah

Acknowledgments

I am indebted to many people for the help, friendship, and tolerance extended to me during the writing of this book. I am especially grateful to all the potters who responded to my research enquiries – I read every word they sent me, and felt awed and uplifted by their generosity. I would particularly like to thank Tim Andrews, Kristin Doner, David Jones, and Rob Sollis for their support.

My thanks, too, to Gus Mabelson, for introducing me to raku; my son Mark for computer graphics; Kerstin Goulding, Angelika Inglis, and Najla Kahli for translations; Harry Fraser, managing director of Potclays Limited, for technical advice; Renee Fairchild of *Ceramics Monthly* for putting me in touch with US potters; Andy McInnes for his continued friendship and support; National Living Treasure Doug Jones, for being himself; and my editors, Linda Lambert and Alison Stace, for their encouragement, trust and support.

This book was written to the music of John Coltrane, Thelonius Monk, Guy Davis and Robert Johnson.

Introduction

Gus Mabelson organised a raku evening for Northampton Potters some 20 years ago. He had a small, highly efficient ceramic fibre kiln, fired with propane, which at that time was unusual in the UK. Around 12 potters glazed and fired the pieces they had brought along. Raku firing is dramatic, especially so at night, but in addition to the atmosphere, I was captivated by both the process and the possibilities. At the end of the evening Gus remarked that I had enough pots for a small exhibition; I still have some.

Since then, although I have worked in other areas of pottery (slipware and reduced stoneware), I have maintained a constant interest in raku, buying all the books on the subject, and keeping a file of photocopied articles. In particular, Tim Andrews' book became a major source of inspiration and comfort.

Raku encourages curiosity and exploration, and I am constantly amazed at the variety and quality of work being created in this medium. The slides potters have sent me pay tribute both to individual artistic endeavour and dedication, and to the achievements in this relatively young genre.

I am very aware of the 400-year history of the Raku family, and work I have seen by the current Mr Raku, Kichizaemon XV, I found especially meaningful. This book, however, is concerned with what might best be called Western raku – the complete metamorphosis of techniques which has occurred in the West over the last 50 years or so, initially in the USA and latterly anywhere potters fire using this method. My working definition of raku stems from this and comes from David Roberts, 'Raku is taking a hot pot from the kiln and doing something to it'.

Apart from a technical definition, it is necessary to be aware of raku as a way of thinking, with an attitude of openness to the unexpected, and a willingness to use accidental happenings in the development of work. Western raku – porous, with non-functional glazes or no glaze at all – has been a liberating influence in ceramics, giving us the freedom to make non-utilitarian objects of beauty and contemplation.

This book is intended as an accessible and practical guide, which will hopefully provide inspiration and direction for further research and creativity. Use the ideas, adapt, change, personalise – make your work your own. Any artistic endeavour should be an expression of yourself, on your own particular journey. It should grow and evolve as you do, and reflect the unique influences on your life.

Chapter One
A Brief History of Raku

There are two chapters in the history of raku – firstly, its origins and development in Japan over a period of 400 years, and secondly, the transfer of the technique to the West in the early part of the last century and its subsequent metamorphosis.

During the Momoyama period in Japan (1573–1615) a potter named Chojiro was charged with making wares for the tea ceremony by the influential tea master Sen-no-Rikyu. Sen-no-Rikyu was tea master to the military dictator of Japan, Toyotomi Hideyoshi, and was responsible for simplifying the tea ceremony, and replacing Chinese pots used in it with others based on unsophisticated Korean wares. His influence on the culture of Japan remains to this day.

The pieces Chojiro produced were, in contrast to the standards of the time, of great simplicity and elegance, and were in keeping with the Zen aesthetics of the tea ceremony. Chojiro's father was originally from China, and is thought to have introduced the techniques of three-coloured glazed pottery to Japan. However, early raku wares were either red or black, and were fired by what we now refer to as the raku process, in which the pots are removed from the kiln whilst red hot.

The title 'Raku' was bestowed upon Chojiro's son Jokei by Hideyoshi in the form of a gold seal. (The word is variously translated as meaning pleasure, enjoyment, contentment, and felicity, and comes from one of the characters in the name of a palace built by Hideyoshi, Jurakudai). 'Raku' in Japan is therefore a family name, a pottery dynasty, though the use of the technique is not restricted to the Raku family. The current holder of the title, Mr. Raku Kichizaemon, is the 15th generation. Work I have seen by him I found intensely moving.

Bernard Leach was responsible for introducing raku to the West. His eloquent description (at the beginning of chapter two in *A Potter's Book*) of his first encounter with raku has changed potters' lives. In it he writes of attending a party in Tokyo in 1911 with other artists and writers, of decorating a pot which was then glazed and fired using the raku process, and of how this so captivated him that he sought and found a teacher, Ogata Kenzan. Leach was taught to make raku and stoneware by Kenzan; the name is a hereditary title, and Kenzan honoured Leach by conferring on him the title of seventh Kenzan.

After a further nine years in the east Leach returned to England and established the pottery at St. Ives in 1920 with Shoji Hamada, and it was here that raku was first practised in the West. There are examples of raku pots made by Hamada at St. Ives before his return to Japan in 1923. Raku firings were later organised to attract visitors to the pottery, with cream teas being served whilst the decorated pots were being fired in an updraught slipware kiln.

Western raku, as a different entity to the Japanese, really began with Paul Soldner's experiments in the USA around 1960. Soldner studied avant-garde ceramics with Peter Voulkos in California. Having read Bernard Leach's description of raku firing he built a portable gas-fired kiln which was used for demonstrations. Disliking the fired glazes, he acted on intuition and rolled the red-hot pots in leaves from a nearby pepper tree. The resulting glaze was more muted, with the suggestion of oxide reduction, and offered the prospect of exciting experimentation. It is this process – the taking of the hot pot from the kiln and doing something to it – that differentiates Western raku from Japanese raku, which is allowed to cool naturally in the air. Some 40 years after Soldner's initial experiments raku potters are equally as intrigued by the possibilities and variations inherent in the technique.

Further Information

For more information on the history of raku I suggest reading the relevant sections in the books by Tim Andrews (which has a major contribution from David Leach, Bernard Leach's son), and David Jones. The Raku Museum website is another good source. (See the Bibliography and website sections at the end of this book).

Chapter Two
Clays for Raku

The principal requirement of a raku clay – beyond the ability to be made into the form which you see in your mind – is that it must be able to withstand the thermal shock involved in the raku process. The rapid heating in the kiln, and the subsequent removal from the fire, subject the work to tremendous stresses. A porous, non-vitrified body is needed to counteract these.

Almost any clay can be used for raku, though some modification may be required. Adding 10–30% grog, sand, or, best of all, Molochite to a clay body (that is, incorporating a proportion of pre-fired material) will significantly increase its resistance to thermal shock,

as will the addition of up to 20% talc. (Molochite is china clay which has been heat treated; it remains the same chemically but no longer holds the properties of a clay). If you are throwing, the additions should be fairly fine, as sharp sand quickly removes layers of skin!

It is, however, a fallacy that raku clay needs to be coarse. Rob Sollis uses a smooth body (50% Molochite 200s mesh, 50% high alumina ball clay) which results in an excellent glaze quality, and burnishes well. Porcelain can be used if care is taken with the

Pots by Rob Sollis, author's collection. *Photograph by John Mathieson.*

firing, which should be from cold, with a slow temperature rise and gentle cooling.

Commercially available raku clays do seem to vary in quality; some are carefully formulated, whilst others are simply stoneware clays with coarse grog or sharp sand added. However, many prepared stoneware clays can be successfully used for raku – my standard clay, DSS from Dobles, is a fairly coarse body which works well. Test the stoneware clays available to you, e.g. check the various suppliers catalogues and request samples (see pp.123–25), and ask for samples from all the potters you know. Don't make the pieces too precious – you will learn more by testing a number of clays and glazes quickly than by investing a great deal of time and energy into a few items. It is vital to mark test pieces accurately, and to keep comprehensive records which you must never, ever lose. You will almost certainly refer back to tests made years ago, and the accumulated knowledge will often provide insights into other problems as they arise.

In the UK, thanks to the work of David Roberts and Tim Andrews, two raku bodies have become standard. David worked for a long time with Potclay's 1106 White St.Thomas' body with 10% grog (20s to dust) added. This is a relatively inexpensive clay which works well for both handbuilding and throwing. Today David and Tim both use a mixture of T-material and porcelain, in David's case in the proportion of 2:1 for handbuilding, while Tim uses equal parts for throwing. Tony White uses T-material without additions for his animal sculptures. T-material is manufactured to a secret recipe by Morganite Thermal, though other companies market less expensive versions. It probably incorporates graded grains of Molochite, and this high proportion of pre-fired material gives low shrinkage and good resistance to thermal shock. It fires white, and burnishes well.

David Roberts coiling, using a mix of T-material and porcelain.

The porosity of a clay, and therefore its resistance to thermal shock, is affected by the biscuit (bisque) firing temperature; the higher the firing, the more vitrified the body, with the degree of vitrification depending on the specific clay being used. Most raku pots are biscuit fired to around 980°C (1790°F), the standard biscuit temperature for studio pottery. There are exceptions to this: Tim Andrews and Peter Powning fire to 1050°C (1920°F), and Horst Kerstan to 1100°C (2010°F). John Wheeldon fires lower, to 950°C (1740°F), and glaze fires at 1000°C (1825°F). In Japan, where raku is traditionally reserved for tea ceremony wares, David Atamanchuk responded to concerns expressed by Japanese buyers regarding the softness of his (non-tea ceremony) pieces by developing a technique which involves biscuit firing to 1150–1200°C (2100– 2190°F).

If the clay you are using is coarse, glaze quality can be improved by using a slip. Because of the generally low-firing temperatures used in raku, slip adhesion can be poor or even almost non-existent if the clays involved are markedly different, as for instance when using an earthenware slip on a high-firing stoneware clay. Using a slip made from your sieved body clay will overcome this problem.

It is worth adding here the comments of Nesrin During, a prominent raku maker featured in this book. She writes: *I think the clay you use for raku is terribly important. One ought to try as many clays as possible until you find your clay and try to get the best results out of that. If the clay is what you want in your hands you can make it fit raku firing by adding grog or sand.*

Paperclay

Paperclay is the name given to a mix of clay and cellulose fibre. It can be used very effectively in raku, especially for large slab forms. Gail Bakutis makes 'wall tablets' up to 90 cm x 65 cm (30 in. x 22 in.) with this material. The cellulose gives the clay a tensile strength it otherwise lacks, enabling large pieces to be handled easily during the firing process. The cellulose burns out in the firing, leaving a relatively light panel, which is easy to hang on walls. Indeed, paperclay can be used for all forms of handbuilding, and wet clay can be added to dry clay with no ill effect.

My suppliers, Top Pot Supplies, recommend a mix of 4:1 clay to wet paper, though up to 1:1 can be used. The paper fibre should be mixed with hand-hot water until it is uniformly damp, when it can be added to clay slip. This can be part-dried on plaster batts or towels for immediate use, or dried completely for storage. Wet paperclay will not store, as mould develops, with accompanying odours. Dried paperclay can be reconstituted easily and quickly by standing a block of it on a wet towel.

Flaxclay

In association with Ian Gregory (author of *Kiln Building*), Scarva Pottery Supplies has developed a range of clays – Scarva TS Flaxclays – which incorporate finely chopped fibres of flax. They say that it has all the benefits of paperclay, but with no mould growth has a much longer shelf life. It is suitable for raku. Through demonstrations Ian has created a great deal of interest in Flaxclay in Europe and the UK.

Right Gail Bakutis, paperclay wall panel, 58 cm x 46 cm x 5 cm (23 in. x 18 in. x 2 in.).

Chapter Three
Making and Decorating Techniques

Making

All the many ways of working with clay and shaping this wonderful material have their place in raku. Handbuilding – modelling, slabbing, coiling, press-moulding, throwing and even slipcasting, can all be used. However, because of the severe stresses involved in the raku process, it is worth paying special attention to several aspects of making:

- Joints must be strong. When teaching, I use the phrase 'scratch, slip and smooth', which is a way to remind my students to *scratch* the surfaces to be joined, to paint thick *slip* onto both surfaces, and then to *smooth* the joint. (Use sieved body clay, coarse particles can disfigure the surface of your work.) The slip is usually essential, but it is not always possible to follow the whole sequence, as some parts of the joins may be inaccessible. With slabs, it is worth making stitchmarks across the joined edges, and to then press thin coils of clay into the angles formed by the slabs. Coiled work alone does not need this treatment, unless handles or decoration are being added, or the pot has partially dried between working sessions.

Joining slabs: scratch and paint slip on the surfaces to be joined, add a coil to the angle formed by the slabs, and compress the outer edges together using stitchmarks. *Computer graphic by Mark Mathieson.*

- Raku-fired clay, being low temperature and therefore 'soft' in ceramic terms, is not very strong, so thin decorative additions may not survive if they are knocked.
- Try to avoid excessive variations in thickness – thicker sections hold the heat of the firing for longer and can cause additional stresses.
- Be aware of the internal dimensions of the kilns you are using – making work too large to either biscuit or raku fire with the facilities available is very frustrating.
- Anticipate how you will remove your work from the raku kiln. You will need a way to lift each piece out with raku tongs, without damaging it or the pots beside it. Bowls are easy to remove but a tile may be more difficult.

And from a more philosophical perspective:

- Observe, absorb, take ideas from different sources, and allow them to evolve into your own statement. To you, it may be obvious where an idea came from – a handle, the curve of a rim – but if you use it in your own way, it becomes an integrated part of your work. Other influences may be difficult or impossible to quantify – landscape and music, for instance. Some potters deliberately avoid looking at ceramics, others research the subject endlessly. Be honest with yourself and above all, choose your own path.
- Be open to new ideas. As with a piece of music or a painting, work you might dismiss now – for whatever reason – may reveal itself to you and enhance your life later. I remember my (sadly negative) reaction when I first saw Mark Rothko's work – now I find his colour fields wonderful.
- Tom Paxton once said, 'When I stop asking questions, I'll be all through'. Ask questions – of potters, of yourself. Most potters are very willing to talk about their work, and to offer encouragement and advice. Potters' fairs are an excellent opportunity to meet potters, and to see a great variety of work; certainly in the UK the standard is usually very high.

Decorating techniques

Slip decoration

Slips can be used in raku to give a smooth surface on a coarser body, and/or to add colour. It is normally applied by dipping, spraying, or brushing. Under a glaze, a slip can result in a smoother finished surface. If the slip is coloured with oxides it will affect the colour of the glaze.

Used without a glaze, slips are usually burnished (that is, polished with the back of a spoon, a smooth pebble, a steel scraper, even a plastic bag) when the clay is leatherhard. This may be done several times, depending on the finish required. In order to avoid marking the pot with the fingers, some potters wear disposable gloves whilst burnishing.

The slip needs to be compatible with the body clay, as the body and slip need to shrink at the same rate in order to create and maintain a strong bond. Some potters use sieved body clay, possibly with the addition of porcelain. I have seen an earthenware slip, which matured at a much lower temperature than the T-material to which it was applied, separate from the body after glaze firing just as the shell lifts from a hardboiled egg. However, adhesion can be improved by adding a small quantity of frit to the slip.

Slip should be mixed with water and allowed to stand overnight before sieving. Using an electric drill with a paint mixer attached can save a lot of time. A powerbreaker is essential if you are using mains electricity.

Terra sigillata

Terra sigillata is simply a slip composed of the very finest clay particles. It gives an especially smooth surface which burnishes well, and which can be very responsive to post-firing treatments. Used in many ancient cultures, it reached its zenith in Roman ceramics; even after close on 2000 years the surface resembles a matt red-brown glaze. Following the Roman occupation of England, most local museums hold examples of this technique.

Terra sigillata is prepared by mixing fine dry clay with water and a deflocculent such as Calgon water softener, sodium hexametaphosphate, or sodium silicate. After allowing this mixture to stand for 48 hours, first the water layer is siphoned off, then the top layer of the remaining slip – this forms the terra sigillata. Some potters repeat this process several times to obtain the finest possible particles. The French potter Pierre Bayle uses soda as the deflocculent and takes only 7 g (0.25 oz) of slip from 1 kg (2 lb 3 oz) of red clay.

And a note of warning – do not add the discarded slip to your clay body as it can have a detrimental effect on its working properties.

Burnishing

Burnishing is polishing leatherhard clay to a shine, usually with a smooth object such as the back of a spoon, a pebble, a plastic bag, or, on the wheel, a steel scraper. Often it is a layer of slip that is burnished, to give a finer surface quality. Burnishing aligns the flat molecules of clay so that they reflect light – the surface can be almost mirror-like. True burnish is lost above about 930°C/ 1706°F but a smooth surface remains to stoneware temperatures. Many potters polish burnished surfaces with wax after the final firing; a quality furniture polish or beeswax works best.

Chapter Four
Biscuit (Bisque) Firing

The purpose of biscuit firing is to change clay into ceramic – that is, to transform the clay, which fragments easily when dry (and which can be recycled), into a hard, strong material that will last indefinitely. In the early stages of the bisque firing, loose water is driven off by the heat. Later, between 450° and 700°C (842° and 1292°F), chemically combined water is lost during the process of ceramic change, after which the clay can no longer be reconstituted.

Clay becomes more vitrified, and therefore stronger but less porous, the higher it is fired. In raku we want a fired body which is strong enough to be handled, yet porous enough both to pick up a good glaze covering and to withstand the thermal shock of the firing process. In practice we find these criteria are usually met by biscuit firing to 980°C (1786°F). Many potters fire to this temperature, partly because it has become standard for biscuit firings for both earthenware and stoneware, and also so that raku pots may be fired in a kiln alongside other work. Most clays fired to this temperature are porous and reasonably strong, although some

David Jones packing the trolley kiln for a biscuit firing. *Photograph by Inax, Japan.*

Rob Sollis unpacking the kiln after a biscuit firing. *Photograph by Alun Tipping.*

earthenwares, particularly local clays, may be close to vitrification. If you find your stoneware clay is very open – easily breakable, porous and 'soft' in ceramic terms – you may wish to fire higher.

Packing

- Pots for firing should be bone dry. Whenever possible I leave thicker pots on top of a firing kiln to ensure they are as dry as possible before packing.
- Place pots on a thin layer of fine sand to allow for expansion and contraction during the firing.
- Pots can touch in the biscuit firing, and can be stacked one on top of another, without problem.

Firing

Any type of kiln can be used for the biscuit firing; whilst the majority of us use an electric kiln for this, the raku kiln itself is perfectly satisfactory.

- Fire *slowly* at the beginning. The critical time during biscuit firing is around 100°C (212°F), when water changes into steam; the resulting sudden increase in pressure can blow your work into thousands of very small pieces. Give the steam time to escape. (From my experience of some 5,000 biscuit firings I do not believe

pots explode in the kiln because of air pockets trapped in the clay.)
- After 150°C (302°F) the rate of temperature rise can be *slowly* increased. Firing is not a race, and there are no prizes for ruined pots. I agree totally with David Jones when he says he fires 'very slowly and cautiously'. You have invested a lot of energy and creativity in your work – why blow it?
- Thicker pots need a slower firing than thinner pieces.
- The vent and spyhole on a kiln should if possible be left open until the temperature has reached 700°C (1292°F).
- As grease from the skin can mark pots and affect glaze adhesion, remove work from the kiln with clean hands.
- *Safety* is always vitally important. Keep people away from a firing kiln, as the outside can become very hot. If possible padlock your kiln door so that it is impossible to open. Don't open the kiln too soon – shelves and bricks retain a lot of heat. If you are kind to your kiln it will last longer.
- If pots are left for some time after the biscuit firing, they should be dusted before glazing.

Single firing

Also known as raw glazing, single firing, as the term implies, means firing a piece of work only once, after it has been glazed in the green state (i.e. glaze applied directly onto the unfired clay). For some potters this offers tremendous advantages – if your anagama kiln takes four days to pack, avoiding having to do this twice could be seen as highly beneficial. In raku, however, where we are normally glaze firing small quantities of work, possibly even single pots, it simply is not practical to wait the minimum of four hours that raw pots need to reach temperature. The one exception to this might be very large pieces which could be single-fired with the kiln built around them. Obviously some experience is required before this should be attempted.

Chapter Five
Glazes and Glazing

Making raku glazes

Raku glazes are not mysterious substances understood only by the initiated. In fact, because they usually consist of only a few ingredients, they can be simple to understand, and consequently easy to experiment with, and alter if necessary.

Any glaze can be used which is designed to melt in the normal raku temperature range, usually 900°–1000°C (1652–1832°F). Many potters mix their own glazes from raw materials, whilst others use commercially available low-temperature glazes.

As a general guide, any low- to mid-temperature frit (the glass-forming part of the glaze), plus 5–20% china clay to give fluidity control, will make a raku glaze. The addition of 1–2% bentonite as a suspension agent will help prevent the glaze settling at the bottom of the bucket. A frit is an industrially-prepared and re-ground substance in which the separate components, which by themselves may be toxic and/or soluble, have been combined into a safe and usable material. For instance, lead oxide is poisonous, but when combined with silica as lead bisilicate it is safe to handle and use in glazes on domestic ware. There are many slipware potters in the UK using lead bisilicate, with beautiful results.

If you look in your supplier's catalogue you will see a number of frits; the company should be able to tell you which are most suitable for raku (and if they can't, change supplier!). As a general guide:

- Lead frits give a transparent glaze with a slight yellow colour and with limited crazing.
- High alkali frits give a clear glaze with extensive fine crazing, and are very responsive with copper carbonate/oxide.
- Soft borax frits give a clear glaze with an open crazing, and are responsive with copper carbonate/oxide.

David Roberts (UK) has developed two glazes which illustrate the difference between alkali and borax frits:

Transparent glaze 1

Soft borax frit	85
China clay	15

This gives an open crazing.

Transparent glaze 2

High alkali frit	85
China clay	15

This give a much finer crazing.

Colour in glazes

The David Roberts transparent glazes previously described will look white, off-white, pink, or darker still, depending on the colour of the clay body underneath. We can bring colour to these glazes by adding either metal oxides or commercially-prepared glaze stains. The colours obtained by the addition of either of these materials depend partly upon the glaze itself, and partly on the

Rob Sollis, *(above)* pouring glaze into a large pot; *(right, above)* plunging a large pot into a bucket of glaze, *(right)* glazing the turned base using a slip-trailer. *Photographs by Alun Tipping.*

treatment given to the work after it has been removed from the raku kiln. A major delight of raku is this lack of predictability, with variations and 'accidents' leading to new areas of exploration.

Oxides

The metal oxides commonly used in raku are:

Tin oxide and zircon Usually both give white; may become grey in reduction. Tin gives the better colour but in the UK is much more expensive than zircon. Usually 5–10% is added to the glaze.

Cobalt oxide/carbonate Gives blue. Usually 0.5–5% is added to the glaze.

Copper oxide/carbonate Is *the* gift to raku potters, producing a wide range of colours from black, through browns, to a range of greens, turquoise, and the metal itself. It is usually used in additions of 3–10%.

Iron oxide Gives iron-red, browns, blacks and yellows. It is usually used in additions of 2–10%.

Manganese dioxide Gives purple-brown and with iron oxide, good blacks. In a lead glaze manganese gives a purple. Usually 4–8% is added to the glaze.

Chrome oxide Gives a strong green. Usually 1–5 % is added to the glaze.

Oxides can be combined in a glaze to achieve different colours. For instance, Gertrud Båge (Sweden) uses 4% tin, 1% cobalt, and 0.5% coarse copper to give a bluish violet glaze with copper spots.

Commercial stains

Industrial research has given us a huge range of colours to explore, and most catalogues have pages of glaze and body stains to tempt us. Usually 5–15% is added to the glaze.

Top Bob Smith, painting glaze onto the foot of a large pot.
Above James Bassett, glazing bugs, Northamptonshire Open Studios demonstration. *Photograph by John Mathieson.*

Copper-matt glazes

Copper-matt glazes can produce some spectacular results, with flashes of brilliant colours resting on top of a black or reddish-brown background. Technically they are almost the opposite of the David Roberts glazes previously mentioned, in that the frit is not the glass-forming component, but is needed to

Top Ellen Rijsdorp, removing glaze from the surface of a disc form; after firing, glaze remaining in the grooves will sparkle against the black of the reduced clay.
Above Ellen Rijsdorp, disc with glazed indented lines and resist slip patterning.

stick the copper oxide (or copper carbonate) to the pot. One example of a copper matt glaze, developed by John Wheeldon (UK), is:

Copper oxide 90
Alkali frit   10

Pat Armstrong (UK) uses a recipe identical to this but with the addition of 2% bentonite and some wallpaper paste (this can go mouldy over time).

Copper-matt glazes can prove fugitive – that is, the colour can sometimes fade

after a time. John Wheeldon's advice is to glaze fire to a higher temperature should this problem occur. This will harden the glaze and make it less susceptible to chemical change. Tim Andrews, who uses a copper-matt glaze with a much higher proportion of frit (see recipes, p.115), comments that 'the method of reduction/oxidation seems to be much more important than any recipe.'

Soluble Salts

Soluble salts (chlorides, sulphates, and nitrates) can be applied to pots in a variety of ways to produce beautiful iridescent effects. Commonly used salts

Below Gertrud Båge, copper-matt jar, height: 16 cm (6¼ in.).
Right Jannie van der Wel, 'Japanese Woman' (detail), copper-matt.

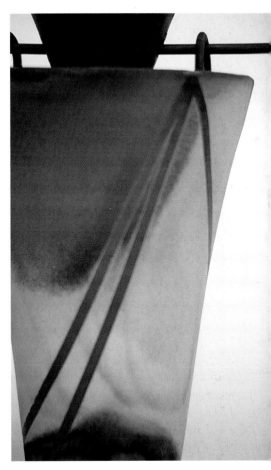

include copper sulphate, barium sulphate, iron sulphate, silver nitrate, and stannous chloride. As they corrode metal, use an inexpensive garden sprayer or, if a more sophisticated spraygun is used, wash immediately after use.

Before firing

A salt solution can be sprayed onto either clay or glaze, or it can be incorporated into a glaze. David Jones (UK) uses silver nitrate in a glaze which gives silver, gold, and yellow:

High alkali frit	50
Lithium carbonate	35
China clay	10
Bentonite	5
Silver nitrate	1.5

Although expensive, even 1% of silver nitrate will give results. Silver nitrate is sensitive to light, so mix only what you need with dry ingredients before adding water. If any glaze remains unused, store it in a lightproof container. David also suggests using photographic waste for spraying.

During firing

Salts can be put directly into the kiln during firing, perhaps in small bowls placed strategically near pots, or poured from a chute onto a piece of clay (to protect the kiln floor) in the firemouth.

The resulting vapours will affect all the pots in the kiln, but experiments will be needed to determine the quantity of materials required, and the length of time needed in the firing.

Left Pat Armstrong, copper-matt vases.
Right Bob Smith, lidded vessel, air-brushed with ferric chloride after removing from the raku kiln, height: 56 cm (22 in.).

Fuming after firing

Salts can be sprayed on the molten surface of the glaze when the red-hot pots are taken from the kiln. Spraying a water-based solution onto a red-hot object is dramatic, and can be very dangerous, so extreme care is needed. However, this approach gives a degree of control in that specific areas can be treated, cooled with a wet cloth to preserve an effect, or given extra reduction with directly applied sawdust. Bob Smith (USA) sprays ferric chloride on his work. (See Chapter Nine, Raku Firing for more details.)

Rick Hirsch (USA) sprays metallic salts on the hot ware 'not to achieve a lustre, but a patina'. He uses ferric

chloride, cupric chloride, and cupric sulphate, with the patina developed during the post-firing reduction.

SAFETY – the above techniques involving soluble salts are potentially very dangerous. The chemicals involved are poisonous so protective breathing equipment is vital. Use rubber gloves and protective clothing.

Wax resist

Wax, either as wax emulsion or hot wax, can be used to create patterns and define areas, both directly onto the pot, and on glaze prior to a second dipping or spraying. Some potters wax the bases of their work to prevent glaze adhering during dipping; personally I think this is more time-consuming than sponging off the excess; and in addition you have the unpleasant smell of burning wax when the pot is fired.

Hot wax gives a better resist but is less convenient to use and tends to ruin your brushes. Wax emulsion should be left to dry for a time to allow the combined water to evaporate. Wet your brushes with water before dipping them in the emulsion, and wash them immediately after use in washing up liquid.

Resist slip

Also known as sacrificial glazing and naked raku, resist slip involves covering the (usually burnished) biscuit-fired pot with a clay slurry, and, when this is dry, dipping the pot in a glaze. During the post-firing process smoke penetrates the crazing in the glaze and passes through the layer of clay to mark the surface of the pot. When the pot is cool the markings are revealed by removing the glaze layer – not unlike shelling a hard boiled egg. Be careful! Edges

of the sections of glaze can cut.

Masking tape, wax resist, and etched lines can all be used to create patterns through the resist slip – where the pot body is exposed will be darker than the areas which remain protected by the slip/glaze layer. Tim Andrews blows air into the glaze to trap bubbles immediately before dipping a pot; the resulting holes in the glaze allow smoke to penetrate and leave a random pattern of dots on the finished piece.

The clay layer needs to adhere to the surface of the pot before firing, but must not permanently attach itself during the firing. To achieve this we use a refractory material, that is, one with a high melting point. David Roberts (UK) gives the following recipe:
China clay   3
Flint   2

Different glazes will give different crackle patterns; again, it is a case of experimenting, of building on information to find an approach which suits your own work.

Tim Andrews (UK) gives this recipe for a resist slip:
China clay   1
Quartz   1
Plus 5–10% aluminium hydroxide to prevent adhesion. He writes: *I have found that the recipe of the slip resist needs to be altered according to the body being used. A more open body needs a slip which will stick well in order to prevent the smoke sneaking in underneath and turning the whole thing black. Timing of the smoking procedure is also a big factor in this. A porcelainous body will tolerate a much longer smoking period than a more open body.*

Tim also adds copper ('maybe 10%') for some colours, particularly when heavily reduced in the kiln, or sugar (a 1 kg/2.2 lb bag in a bucket) which can produce some good smoke effects; both tend, however, to make the slip more difficult to remove after the firing.

Susan Luker (UK) uses the same resist slip as David Roberts (3 china clay with 2 flint) which she pours over the pot. She often uses this over a latex resist, applied in selected areas which, after peeling away, allows the surface of the pot to be painted with glaze.

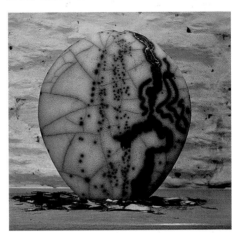

Top right Susan Luker, resist slip on biscuit-fired vase – note latex resist.
Middle left Peeling latex resist from the vase. *Middle right* Painting copper glaze onto areas of the vase previously protected by the latex resist. *Bottom left* Vase ready for firing, showing slip-resist and glazed areas. *Bottom right* Finished fired vase, with shelled resist slip.

Above Kristin Doner, pillow pots, slip resist, 13 cm x 8 cm (5 in. x 3 in.). *Photograph by Hap Sakwa, Sabastopol, California.*

Commercial Glazes

Many suppliers produce a base glaze and/or a range of raku glazes. Commercial earthenware glazes in the range 900°–1050°C (1652°–1922°F) can be ideal for raku. Jola Spytkowska (UK) uses 'brush-on' earthenware glazes – excellent for painting different areas of her small and brightly coloured 'creatures'.

As with a glaze mixed from raw

materials, adding 1–2% bentonite to a commercial glaze will prevent it from caking in the bottom of the container.

Notes on Materials

Gerstley borate

Gerstley borate, widely used in raku glaze recipes, especially by Americans, ceased to be mined in the USA in 2000. Some potters' suppliers still hold small stocks. Harry Fraser, managing director of Potclays Limited in the UK, tells me he is evaluating Gillespie borate and Murray borate, both of which have been synthesised in the USA to match Gerstley, and will select one as a replacement. The Laguna Clay Company in California markets Laguna borate as a substitute. Plainsman Clays Ltd. in Medicine Hat, Alberta, markets Boraq, a substitute devised by on-going experimentation by potters. More information can be found on the Gerstley borate website (see p.126).

Jola Spytkowska, 'Mr & Mrs', height: 30.5 cm (12 in.).

Copper oxide and copper carbonate

These ingredients can be used interchangeably in glaze recipes; however, the carbonate is weaker than the oxide and you may need to add more.

In my experience the carbonate is the finer of the two, and is considerably cheaper in the UK. It gives a green colour to the glaze mix (the oxide is black) – useful in a teaching situation to make the glaze identifiable.

Mixing glazes

Always label your raw materials with a waterproof marker.

The raw materials for your glaze should be weighed out on scales and added to water in a bucket. It is better to have too little water than too much, as it is easier to add more than to siphon off. In addition, some frits are slightly soluble, so you will lose material if you have to siphon. Stir the glaze thoroughly, then leave it overnight before sieving through an 80s mesh. Allowing the glaze to sit enables the materials to soften, making sieving so much easier. I use a nylon washing-up brush and a rubber kidney when sieving, though recently I've taken to using a paint mixer attachment on an electric drill to mix the glaze beforehand, and I've found it to be very quick and effective. *A powerbreaker is essential if you are using mains electricity.*

The procedure is the same for a commercially prepared glaze, except of course no weighing of separate ingredients is involved, although you may find it necessary to add 1–2% bentonite to prevent settling.

- To check if a glaze is the right

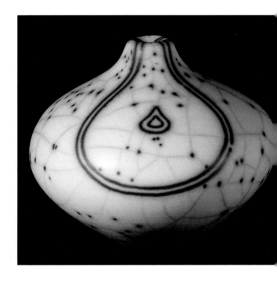

Tim Andrews, eliptical gourd, slip resist, dia: 41 cm (16 in.). *Photograph by Sam Bailey.*

  consistency for glazing, dip your finger into it – you should just be able to see the wrinkles on your skin through the glaze.
- Label glaze buckets clearly with a waterproof marker. I have found it useful to include the recipe on the label; it is often quicker to find the bucket than to find your notes.
- Keep written records of all your glazes, tests, experiments and results. You never know when you might need to refer to something you did long ago. Again, write your notes in a waterproof pen and keep them somewhere safe.
- When weighing out materials, tick off each material *and* each quantity of that material as it goes into the bucket. It is very easy to get distracted after weighing out, for example, 3 of the 5 kg (11 lb) of frit needed for a glaze. A phone call, a conversation, daydreaming, can all make you lose the ability to count up to five. Mixing

glazes is a necessary but fairly boring activity, and you need to get it right.

- *Safety* – when handling dry materials *always* wear a face mask. Your supplier should be able to recommend a mask that complies with the health and safety requirements of your country. Ceramic materials vary in the dangers they present, but inhaling fine particles of any kind is not good for the health. Wipe up any spills and dispose of the residue safely. Do not eat, drink, or smoke in the workshop. Wash your hands after you have handled ceramic materials.

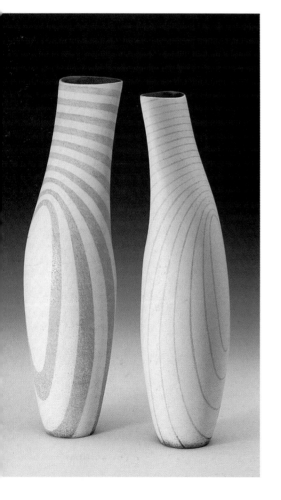

Applying Glazes

Glazes can be applied by dipping, pouring, spraying, or painting onto the pot, or any combination of these methods.

Dipping

This is the most used method of glazing, with the advantage of giving an even coating of glaze to the pot. If a container is being glazed, the inside is usually done first, and the pot allowed to dry for a short time before the outside is dipped. Double dipping using glazes of different colours can give interesting results, but be careful not to create a glaze layer which is so thick that it will either pull away from the pot as it dries, or run off the pot in the kiln.

Pouring

Pouring glaze over your pot can result in areas of different thickness, adding interest to your work. Different colours can be used for further effect.

Spraying

Using either a single glaze, or glaze-on-glaze, subtle gradations of colour can be obtained by spraying. Some specialist equipment is needed – Jim Bassett uses a basic spraygun and compressor he bought for £90 (US$125) from a machine tool supplier. Ideally – for health reasons – a spraybooth with extractor fan should be used, and a face mask is essential.

David Roberts, 'Two Tall Vessels With Ellipses', coil-built, slip resist, height: 59 cm (23 in.).

Painting

Painting can be used in a variety of ways to highlight areas of a piece of work, to emphasise features, or simply to add variety and create opportunities for happenings in the kiln. Painting onto large areas requires either commercial 'brush-on' glazes, which spread to give an even coat before drying, or several layers of glaze.

Cleaning the base

To prevent your work sticking to the kiln shelf during the firing, after you have finished glazing clean both the base of your work and 7mm (¼ in.) up the sides. Use a damp sponge with a clean edge for this.

For health reasons, clean the glazing area thoroughly using a sponge and plenty of water.

David Jones, spraying glaze. Note masking tape used to delineate areas. *Photograph by Inax, Japan.*

Time and iridescence

Over a period of time the iridescence on your work may fade, the metals (which are on the surface, and not part of the glaze structure) combining with gases in the atmosphere to lose their shine. You can have a zen-like attitude and accept this softening of the colours as part of the process, or you may prefer to pre-empt it by sealing the pot with a wax or silicone polish.

Firing different glazes together

As it is likely that glazes using different frits will mature at different temperatures, I suggest firing seperately. Otherwise you may need to remove pots which have reached temperature, and then continue firing.

Chapter Six
Kilns – Fuel and Construction Materials

The kiln is the focus of the ceramic process. All the many aspects of working with clay contribute to the final result, from the research and inspiration, through the making processes, even to such mundane duties as sieving glaze. But it is the kiln which transforms your efforts and aspirations – into what? I think most experienced potters would expect 'satisfactory' results from their firings, and would be prepared for some pieces to fail, perhaps technically, perhaps by their artistic standards. But sometimes – when the kiln god smiles, and all contributing factors have harmonised in just the right way – something special emerges from the kiln that goes beyond what you could have expected and brings a particular pleasure to your work.

People have different reactions to seeing work as it comes out of the firing, from dancing around to being quietly subdued. It is particularly important to remember that your first response to a fired piece may not be your final, considered evaluation. Months later you can find qualities in your pots that you missed at first – good and bad! Discuss your work with people whose opinions you respect – they may see what you have missed and suggest possible developments that you have not considered.

In practical terms, a kiln is a structure which contains heat, sufficient heat to melt the raku glaze. So that pots can be removed easily, the interior needs to be accessible – or conversely, the kiln itself must be light enough to lift off. It needs to be placed close to the reduction chamber. *Safety* must always be a major consideration – carrying a red-hot pot is potentially extremely hazardous, and the risk of fire is ever-present.

To obtain the necessary heat, we have

David Atamanchuk; heating pots to 1000°C (1832°F) on the top shelf of an electric kiln: (*right*) reducing by wrapping newspaper round the pot.

a choice of fuel, and consequently a choice of kiln.

Electric kilns

Katherine Pleydell-Bouverie described electricity as 'a good servant'. Not many raku potters use it, perhaps because part of the intrigue of raku lies in the flame – potters are often described as pyromaniacs! However, it should not be dismissed – to gain an idea of the standard that can be reached with electricity, look at the work of Peter Powning (Canada), Horst Kerstan (Germany), and David Atamanchuk (Canada/Japan). Peter uses a range of five digitally-controlled kilns and has a large air-to-air heat exchanger to recover the heat from them and so warm the building. (In the New Brunswick winter this is of real benefit and environmentally helpful). The pots are allowed to cool to around 700°C (1292°F) before being removed from the kiln and reduced in sawdust or shredded newspaper. Horst fires in a small electric kiln which holds six tea bowls. David writes: 'The electric kiln gives me even heat and is easy to control, automatically switching off at 1000°C (1832°F)'.

He fires about 18 pots on the top shelf only of a top-loading kiln.

This brings us to the question of *safety.* Firstly, it is *essential* to have an automatic cut-off on the door of an electric kiln. Live elements can kill. Secondly, electric kilns are located indoors – the heat released when the door or lid is opened could be a serious burn risk to the operator, and a serious fire risk to the building. Thirdly – how close is the reduction container, and are there any hazardous obstacles between it and the kiln?

Gas kilns and burners

Allied to the development of ceramic fibre insulation material, the availability of bottled LPG – liquefied petroleum gas – has been a major contributory factor to the growing popularity of raku. It is the fuel used by the majority of raku potters. A propane gas cylinder is relatively cheap and will last a number of firings, depending on size. I use large 47 kg (104 lb) bottles at home, and 19 kg (42 lb) if I have to take the bottle in the car – it's much kinder to my back, and to the car! *Note* – LPG is sold commercially as propane and butane. As gas is drawn from the cylinder, the remaining liquid cools and the evaporation rate slows; for the raku potter the practical difference between the two fuels is that butane will not turn from liquid to gas below 0°C (32°F), while propane can be used at much lower temperatures. Butane tends to be used for low-pressure domestic appliances indoors, and outdoors during the summer – it is the gas used, for instance, in barbecues. Because of their much higher pressure, and for obvious safety reasons, propane cylinders should *always* be stored outdoors.

For firing with a cylinder of gas you

The author's Bullfinch 1260 burner and tongs.

will need a burner with a handle incorporating an on-off valve, 2 m (6.6 ft) of hose, and a gas regulator. Your supplier will be able to give advice regarding the size of burner you need for your size of kiln. A flame-failure device (thermal cutout) is advisable, especially in an educational situation.

I use a single Bullfinch 1260 burner with a tough flat-sided nylon handle which allows the burner to be secured during firings with a brick – steel spring handles are stronger but, being round in section, are more liable to move. The burner nozzle is 4.8 cm (1⅞ in.) in diameter. This assembly cost me £80 (US$112); a thermal cutout would have added £15 (US$21). I direct the burner at an angled firebrick which acts as a 'flame divider' to circulate the heat more effectively within the kiln. David Jones uses two opposed burners with 2.5 cm (1 in.) diameter nozzles in a kiln 56 cm (22 in.) wide and which varies in height from 13 cm (5 in.) to 81 cm (31 in.). This gives a relatively slow firing for the tallest kiln size, but the work being fired is large, and so needs more cautious treatment.

Wood kilns

Wood is the traditional fuel used by raku potters. When, in the early 1920s, Bernard Leach first introduced the technique to the West, in St Ives, Cornwall, he fired with wood, helped by a paraffin drip. (For a full account of raku at St Ives, read David Leach's contribution to Tim Andrews' book – see the Bibliography.)

Wood firing has tended to be eclipsed by the convenience of bottled gas. However, Nesrin During (Denmark), seeking effects obtainable only by wood firing, never takes more than one hour to reach temperature, using an updraught kiln; subsequent loads take only 15 to 20 minutes. If you have a plentiful supply of wood available, and a safe place to build your kiln where the smoke will not annoy your neighbours, this method of firing should be seriously considered. And the ash residue in the firebox can be given to a potter who works in stoneware, to make into a high-temperature glaze!

Oil kilns

I must confess that I have never actually seen an oil-fired raku kiln. However, there is plenty of information available regarding oil firing and suitable burners in books on kiln construction. As a fuel it necessitates a more complex set-up than either wood or gas, but in your situation it may be the ideal source of heat, and if it's already in place, go for it!

Insulation materials

Ceramic fibre

The development of ceramic fibre gave potters a lightweight, easy to use, and highly efficient insulating material which is not affected by thermal shock. It is available in varying thickness and grades (relating to maximum firing temperature) of blanket, board and paper, and in pre-formed units. Blanket is very adaptable – it is easy to make a kiln which suits the size and shape of your work with it, or to use it to insulate an available container such as an oil drum or an oven. It can even be used for one-off kiln construction, for instance wrapped around a large sculptural item. Board can likewise be used in many aspects of kiln construction, but it is easily damaged and needs support. Small pieces of board are very useful in reducing flue size during firing.

Moulded vacuum-formed sections are light, pre-shrunk and dust-free if given an alumina wash, and highly efficient. Cylinders are the most useful shape for a raku kiln.

Health and safety – *Always wear a face mask when handling ceramic fibre.* In 1998 alumina-silica ceramic fibre blanket was classified as a Grade 2 carcinogen. In experiments with laboratory animals it had been shown to cause serious health problems, including

Below Ceramic fibre kiln built by Gail Bakutis at Rufford Ceramic Centre. *Photograph by John Mathieson.*
Right Gail Bakutis removing hot pots from the Rufford kiln. *Photograph by John Mathieson.*

lung cancer. Since then, newer, safer ceramic fibres have been introduced:

- high alumina fibres (e.g. Saffil, Maftek) – these are expensive.
- stabilised-silica fibres (e.g. Superwool, Carbowool). These have a chemistry and a mean average fibre diameter which allows solubility in the lung, and hence removal from the body over a reasonable time period. Known as 'body-soluble'.

I am grateful to Harry Fraser, managing director of Potclays Limited, for this information.

Firebricks

Firebricks are quite expensive to buy new, but can sometimes be obtained second-hand, or rescued from a defunct electric kiln. A permanent structure can be built using cement, but dry-building is perfectly satisfactory, especially if it is made safer by using some form of angle-iron frame to hold the shape.

Housebricks

Housebricks can be used for temperatures up to 1000°C (1832°F), though being much more dense than kiln insulating bricks they will take longer to reach temperature. The more open – sandy and porous – the brick, the more suitable it is for our purpose. Do not use vitrified bricks, and do not use bricks made from concrete. The bricks need to be completely dry to prevent spalling (the breaking away of pieces of the heated surface of the brick, sometimes violently). A kiln could be built using housebricks for the base and walls, and insulated on the inside and the roof with ceramic fibre, in which case it could be fired higher than 1000°C (1832°F).

Durox

Ian Gregory (author of *Kiln Building*, a companion volume in this series) has discovered through experimentation an alternative, and cheap, source of kiln insulation. He tested different types of building blocks obtained from local builders' merchants, some of which did not perform well. However, one material, marketed in the UK under the trade name of Durox, has proved ideal.

Durox is composed of a mixture of silica, sand, cement, lime, and aluminium

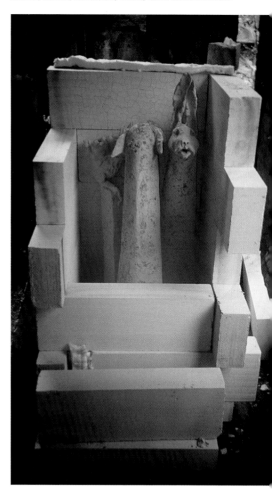

Durox kiln built by Ian Gregory.

powder, and is available in block form, from around the size of a brick to 60 cm x 30 cm x 10 cm (24 in. x 12 in. x 4 in.). The blocks are light in weight, and easy to cut with a saw. An 8 cu. ft (0.23 m³) kiln can be dry-built for as little as £20 (US$28). Ian has found that Durox blocks will withstand temperatures of up to 1100°C (2012°F), which makes them ideal for biscuit firing and for raku. He recommends that the hotface (where the flame hits the kiln wall) be made from solid kiln bricks or HTIs (High Temperature Insulating Bricks). The largest kiln Ian has built with Durox was 70 cu. ft (2 m³).

Ian recommends coating the blocks with ITC (available from Scarva Pottery Supplies in the UK); this will protect from crumbling and give a longer life.

Testing kiln-build material

Materials such as Durox need to be tested in a kiln to at least the temperature to which you will be firing. Remember that what you are testing may shatter and/or melt, damaging other work, the kiln shelves, or even the kiln walls. I suggest that you place a sample of the material in a biscuit-fired lidded container with thick walls – thick because some substances will eat through ceramic, as anyone who has fired clay with a piece of metal, such as a coin, embedded in it will know. The test containers can be quickly made – we aren't looking for artistic perfection here.

ın Construction

Top-loading oil drum kiln

In my research for this book I was surprised how many raku potters use an oil drum as the basis for their kiln. These include Andrew Mason, Ellen Rijsdorp, Jannie van der Wel, Tony White, and Susan Luker. There are several reasons for the drum's popularity – an oil drum is a strong container and will last indefinitely; it is a convenient size, and can be moved relatively easily; it gives flexibility in that it can be cut down and the rings retained to increase kiln height when necessary, and it can be easily insulated with ceramic fibre (see also p. 34–5). My own kiln is made from an oil drum and it has seen many years of service.

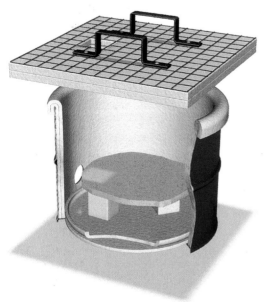

The oil drum should be new – fumes given off from burning chemical residues are potentially harmful. If you are cutting the drum down, think carefully about the maximum height of the pots you will be firing, and add a little to this figure as the fibre roof can sag. You will also need to add the thickness of the ceramic fibre at the bottom of the kiln, and the height of the kiln shelf plus supporting bricks above this – around 12.5 cm (5 in.) in total.

Cutting round an oil drum takes time and patience, but your rewards are a kiln shell the size you want (and an aching arm!). A 57 cm (22½ in.) diameter drum has a circumference of 1.8 m (71 in.). The easy way to cut this distance is to search the Yellow Pages under 'metal' for a workshop with a suitable industrial cutter. To cut it yourself, you have the choice of tinsmith's shears, a hacksaw, or sheet metal cutters. I used Monodex cutters, similar to pliers in construction, which take a small bite with each scissor-like movement. A hole needs to be drilled in order to start cutting.

To avoid cutting both yourself and future damage to the ceramic fibre, the rough cut edge of the drum needs to be smoothed. Wear gloves and start with a file, progressing to silicone carbide ('wet

Design for an oil drum kiln. Note brick angled to divide the flame. *Computer graphic by Mark Mathieson.*

and dry') paper, initially wrapped around a sanding block. The smoother and more rounded the edge, the longer your ceramic fibre blanket will last. In fact, this process – using the proper tools – should not take long.

You will need a burner port 9 cm (3½ in.) in diameter or 5 cm (2 in.) square, cut 9 cm (3 ½ in.) above the base, and a 5 cm (2 in.) spyhole halfway up the side. Round holes can be cut by drilling in a consecutive line, followed by smoothing with a file. Square burner port and spyhole may be easier shapes to tackle, in which case drill holes to mark the corners, and saw between them. Again, smooth off the cut edges.

The roof of the kiln can be made from either the oil drum lid, or from welded mesh. I originally used the lid, but I found that the weight eventually damaged the fibre rim of the kiln body. Recently I replaced this with 5 cm (2 in.) welded mesh, which is both light and strong. You will need to cut a flue – 12.5 cm (5 in.) diameter in the lid, or 10 cm x 10 cm (4 in. x 4 in.) in the mesh. (The flue can be cut larger than required, and reduced in size during firings with a piece of ceramic fibre board.)

Handles – large enough to be held whilst wearing thick gloves – can be made from strap iron (2.5 cm x 0.3 cm/1 in. x 0.1 in. in section), heated and bent to shape, and secured with bolts and large reinforcing washers. They should be placed away from the flue. It is also useful to have handles on the kiln itself.

Ceramic fibre blanket is supplied as a roll. I prefer to use two layers, so for this type of kiln I would add together the requirements for wall, floor and roof and double the total. Make sure the roll you buy is wide enough to cover the height of the kiln wall *plus* at least 5 cm (2 in.) overlap at the top.

The correct size of circle for the base can be obtained by pressing the oil drum onto the blanket, which can be cut easily with scissors. With one base layer in position, place the roll of blanket in the drum and line the wall with a double layer, plus a small (7.5 cm/3 in.) overlap. Protect the base layer with newspaper or a sheet of cardboard while doing this. The second base layer can then be put in place – it will help support the fibre wall.

Ceramic fibre can be secured in place with adhesive (from your supplier), or with ceramic buttons, held in place with nichrome wire. The buttons can be bought, or you can make them yourself. The nichrome wire needs to loop through two small holes drilled in the oil drum – do not overtighten.

The layer of blanket protruding from the top of the kiln should be cut down-wards at 10 cm (4 in.) intervals, lapped over the rim, and held in place with strong (not plasticised) wire.

A double layer of fibre needs to be securely attached to the lid, either with adhesive or buttons. If you are using mesh, a layer of the strongest available kitchen foil, placed between the mesh and the blanket with the shiny side towards the fibre, helps retain heat and prevent damage to the blanket. Burner port, spyhole and flue need to be cut through the blanket. Rigidiser (from your supplier) can be painted on the fibre, stiffening it and so preventing it from becoming easily damaged. However, I have only ever used it on flues and ports. It is advisable not to use rigidiser where you want a good seal, eg. where the lid sits on the kiln.

Extra height can be added to the kiln by utilising the cut-off section of the oil drum as an extension ring. A double layer of ceramic fibre, with overlaps at both the top and the bottom, needs to be

secured to the metal; this simply sits on the kiln wall.

Remember always to wear a breathing mask and gloves when handling ceramic fibre.

The kiln shelf is a discarded ceramic batt made to fit with a hammer and chisel – and I always wear goggles. However, you could use a circular batt, leaving a 3–5 cm (1 ¼ –2 in.) gap between the shelf and the kiln wall. The shelf sits on three firebricks on the bottom of the kiln. I direct the flame at the corner of the brick furthest away from the burner port; this acts as a flame divider, spreading the heat more effectively through the kiln.

Lift-off oil drum kiln

Rob Sollis, Peter Hayes, and David Roberts all use lift-off oil drum kilns. Essentially this is an inversion of the top-loading design above, with the body of the drum being lowered over the work to be fired. It has advantages when firing larger pieces, as they do not need to be moved when hot, but can be reduced in situ by placing a container around them. Peter Hayes has a circular arrangement – like a rotary clothes-line – with which he lifts off

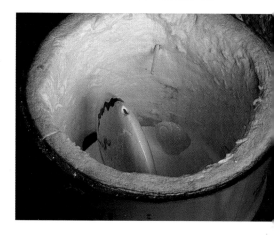

Top Andrew Mason's oil drum kiln.
Above Jannie van der Wel's oil drum kiln.
Right Looking into Susan Luker's red-hot oil drum kiln.

40

and swings away the kiln when the work has reached temperature. It is replaced by the reduction container which is lowered over the piece, to be followed by a plastic refuse bag full of sawdust which remains suspended. This melts with the rising heat, the sawdust drops onto the work, and a lid is put on. With the accompanying smoke and flames, it's a great demonstration, as anyone who has seen Peter perform at Art in Action (near Oxford, UK) or at the National Ceramics Festival (at Hatfield House, UK) will confirm.

The oil drum needs to be lowered and lifted using pulleys, steel cables or chain, (never rope, which can burn), and a counterweight (usually a bucket of sand). The pulley system has to be

Right Rob Sollis's lift-off oil drum kiln.
Photograph by Alun Tipping.
Below Bob Smith's double lift-off oil drum kiln, supported by a child's swing stand.

supported by a frame – you *cannot* take risks when lifting the red hot body of the kiln, so the whole structure *must* be strong and safe.

Potters using a lift-off system normally build the base and firemouth of the kiln with firebricks, perhaps adding ceramic fibre for extra insulation. Partly to make a good seal, and partly to prevent damage to the bottom edge of the insulated drum, ceramic fibre should be used where the kiln body sits on the base. A flue needs to be cut at the top of the kiln.

When loading this type of kiln, it is necessary to allow for the possible

swaying of the kiln as it is lowered and lifted – don't pack too close to the sides.

Metal mesh kiln

Metal mesh offers great potential for building raku kilns. It is easy to work with, gives a choice of rigidity or flexibility, is light to handle, and is relatively inexpensive. I recently bought a sheet of rigid mesh 1800 in. x 1200 m (71 in. x 47 in.) with a 5 cm (2 in.) grid for £20 (US$28). It can be used to make any shape you might need to fire your work. For instance, if you make wide, flat panels, you can make a wide, flat kiln specifically for these. For suppliers – check your Yellow Pages under 'metal'.

Rigid mesh provides a stronger structure than flexible mesh; it will be a little heavier, but more durable, and you will probably be restricted to a flat-sided kiln. A lighter gauge offers greater mobility, and can be curved to form a cylinder. If you particularly want a very light structure, for instance to use as a lift-off kiln without pulleys etc., a very light mesh could be secured to a frame made from 6 mm (¼ in.) diameter steel rod.

A circular or square kiln can be constructed along the lines of the top-loading oil drum kiln described above. Lynda Harris in New Zealand uses a circular kiln of this type. The sections or ends of the mesh panels can be held together with wire; ceramic fibre should be attached to the mesh using nichrome wire and ceramic buttons. The base of a lift-off kiln can be either a firebrick enclosure with a burner port, or fibre can be used to make a base with or without low walls.

Kristin Doner has a lightweight lift-off kiln constructed with mesh, which she

Lynda Harris's top-loading mesh kiln.

places over one of two firing positions situated side by side on a bed of sand, each consisting of a kiln shelf on three firebricks. Her work remains on this shelf after the firing – she reduces each piece under a large bin which she inverts over the firing station.

John Wheeldon has a rigid mesh 'flat-pack' raku kiln (based on Ian Gregory's original design), which he uses for demonstrations. The sides are held together at the corners with heavy-duty clips.

Firebrick gas-fired kiln

It is relatively simple to build a top-loading raku kiln using new or recycled firebricks, perhaps from a redundant kiln. You will need a flat base, such as a kiln shelf or paving slab large enough for the kiln you are building, or a layer of sand. The walls are dry-built onto this base, although for a more permanent structure they could be supported at the corners by angle-iron, held in place with wire tied top and bottom around the kiln. The floor of the kiln can be firebrick or a layer of ceramic fibre blanket. You will need to leave a burner port and spyhole in the walls. Should you need to do so, firebrick is easy to cut with a saw, but always wear a face mask.

The kiln shelf should rest on three firebricks, with the brick furthest from the burner angled to divide the flame.

It is possible to make a roof from fire-brick supported on long bolts attached to angle-iron, but it is easier to use ceramic fibre on rigid mesh, as described in the section on the top-loading oil drum kiln. To make the heat travel and therefore work as much as possible, the flue should be above the burner port – the flame goes under the shelf, is spread by the flame divider and then goes around

Top Kristin Doner's lift-off mesh kiln. Note the two firing positions.
Above John Wheeldon's flat-pack kiln, photographed at the National Pottery and Ceramics Festival, Hatfield House. *Photograph by John Mathieson.*

43

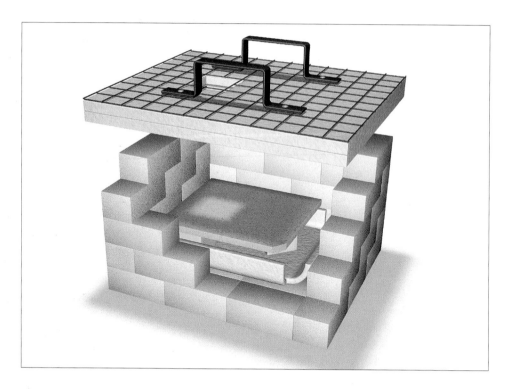

Brick built kiln. Note brick angled to divide the flame which enters the kiln from the left. *Computer graphic by Mark Mathieson.*

the pots to exit at the point furthest from the burner.

A variation on this kiln would be to incorporate the shelf into the walls, with a gap opposite the burner port. The flame would then travel under the shelf and across the pots – what is known as a 'cross-draught' kiln.

Nesrin During's wood-fired kiln

Nesrin has designed a simple, adaptable wood-burning kiln which she has fired many times. It takes some 45 minutes to build, and will reach a temperature of 900°C (1652°F) in never more than an hour, with subsequent loads taking 15

to 20 minutes.

She writes 'The firing results are *always* unique. Not all are beautiful, but some are *very* beautiful, and never boring.'

For the kiln she uses:
- 40–50 dry, porous housebricks (*not* concrete bricks)
- A square kiln shelf
- A metal grill for the grate (from a dump)
- A piece of sheet iron (also from a dump)
- Some broken pieces of kiln shelf

The kiln is built when and where needed, with the firemouth facing into the prevailing wind. Nesrin levels the surface with soil, which also protects whatever is underneath – concrete will crack with excessive heat. The dimensions of the kiln are dictated by the size of the kiln shelf, which sits diagonally across the

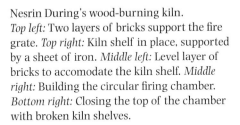

Nesrin During's wood-burning kiln.
Top left: Two layers of bricks support the fire grate. *Top right:* Kiln shelf in place, supported by a sheet of iron. *Middle left:* Level layer of bricks to accomodate the kiln shelf. *Middle right:* Building the circular firing chamber. *Bottom right:* Closing the top of the chamber with broken kiln shelves.

walls. Two courses of bricks are laid to form the back and side walls, with the grate sitting on these. Another two courses are laid, and the kiln shelf placed diagonally across with the walls supporting three corners. The piece of sheet iron (angle-iron can be used) goes across the front of the kiln and supports the fourth corner of the shelf.

45

Nesrin During's wood-burning kiln; firing the kiln, with pots drying on top.
Below Nesrin During giving a firing demonstration.

The remainder of the kiln is built in a circular pattern which gets smaller as the height increases. As some of the bricks stand on the kiln shelf, Nesrin raises the height of the others using pieces of broken shelves. The top is partially closed with broken shelves, leaving a hole in the centre as the chimney.

Nesrin uses scrap wood, dry and thinly split. (Wood needs to be completely dry to realise its full calorific value.) After the bricks have been heated she uses less wood, and rakes the fallen ashes from under the grate to help maintain the flow of oxygen. Pots are placed on top of the kiln to dry. In a teaching situation Nesrin will often use two kilns and fire 'an incredible amount of work'. During the firing bricks can be moved to alter the direction of the flame. When the glaze is mature she removes a few bricks from one side of the kiln in order to remove the pots.

The fuel, the particular results, and

Nesrin During, wood-fired coil pot.
Below Rick Foris' recycled electric kiln.

the lack of expense have combined to create great interest in this kiln. The only problem that Nesrin has heard of was caused by a kiln being built with too small a firemouth for the size of chamber.

Recycled kilns

Some potters have modified redundant electric kilns to use for raku – top-loaders are particularly suitable for this. After removing the elements, a burner port needs to be cut. If the lid is no longer serviceable a replacement can be made with mesh and ceramic fibre.

Rick Foris uses 'an old dead electric kiln body'. He built a firebox beneath it, and replaced the lid with ceramic fibre. Firing with propane he reaches a temperature of 950°–1000°C (1742°–1832°F) in about 30 minutes.

Anna Eilert firing with her commercially-made kiln.

Commercial kilns

If you don't want the hassle of building your own kiln, there are a number of commercial suppliers who offer a variety of different raku kilns – top-loading, lift-off, some even with a gantry. Some are more reasonably priced and offer better value than others. If you decide to buy a kiln, factors you should consider are:

1. Buy the biggest kiln you can afford. As you get more proficient, both your output and the size of your work will increase.
2. When considering the internal dimensions of a kiln, remember that you will lose 10–12.5 cm (4–5 in.) of the stated height because of the bricks and shelf sitting on the kiln floor.
3. Do you want to biscuit fire in your raku kiln?
4. Having the most expensive and shiniest kiln will not improve the work!

Chapter Eight
Health and Safety

There are a number of safety factors to be considered in ceramics, and – because of the direct involvement with fire – even more with raku. I don't want to create unnecessary alarm – most are simply common sense – but it really is essential, both for your own longterm good health and that of those working with you, that proper precautions are taken.

Raw materials

Some of the materials we use in ceramics are directly damaging to our health, such as copper carbonate, which is poisonous, and manganese dioxide, which attacks the nervous system. Others can have debilitating results over a very long period – the inhalation of silica dust can lead to silicosis. Indeed, we should be wary of inhaling *any* dust.

In the workshop we should observe the following rules:

1. Label **all** material containers with a waterproof marker as soon as they reach your studio. The printed labels fade over time, the glue dries and they fall off. Some ceramic materials are easily identifiable – talc for instance – but many are white or off-white in colour, and easily confused.
2. **Always** wear a face mask when handling dry materials. Your supplier will be able to advise you which sort – some do not filter out the finest particles found in a pottery studio.
3. Always close and seal containers of raw materials.
4. Wipe up any spilled materials.
5. **Never** eat, drink, or smoke in the workshop.
6. Wash your hands after leaving the workshop.

Firing

A burn is a terrible injury – when firing we must do everything possible to prevent this happening.

1. Select a safe area for the firing, away from buildings, combustible materials, people and pets. Allow plenty of space for your activities.
2. If you are demonstrating, demarcate the firing area in some way so that it is clear where the public can safely stand and watch.
3. Have a hose-pipe and buckets of water available in case of fire.
4. Plan for the processes and movements involved in firing. You should not be lifting red-hot pots over the rubber hose from the propane cylinder. Keep the ground where you are working free from clutter.
5. Wear protective clothing and non-slip, sturdy shoes. To raku-fire with bare legs is worse than stupid.
6. A face mask and safety gloves are essential when loading and unloading the kiln.
7. Always turn off the gas before opening the kiln.

8. Never leave the kiln unattended.
9. Before finally leaving the firing site make sure nothing is left smouldering.

I don't want to frighten unnecessarily – most of us live with dangerous substances and equipment in our domestic lives and never come to any harm. It's simply that with some care and forethought accidents can be avoided. Also, what is obvious to you, the potter, may not be so to the casual observer. At a private firing I once prevented someone picking up a pot just out of the kiln and cooling prior to being placed in the reduction chamber. It didn't look hot, but her hands would never have recovered had I not stopped her.

Chapter Nine
Raku Firing

David Roberts defines raku as 'taking the hot pot from the kiln and doing something to it'. It is this action which separates raku from all other ceramic processes and makes it unique.

Tools

Raku tongs are essential. They can be bought from potter's suppliers, or you can make them yourself from 6 mm (¼ in.) steel rod. This can be heated and bent to shape, hammered flat at the pivot, and secured with a rivet or small bolt. Some potters shape the jaws specifically to suit the pots they make. My own tongs were made for me by a student in the metal workshop at the school where I was teaching.

Tough gloves or mitts are necessary

Below Pot firing in Rick Foris' kiln. Note the broken pieces of soft firebrick which act as a flame baffle and eliminate hot-spots.
Right Rick Foris, removing a hot pot from his recycled kiln. *Photographs by Mary Jo Pfankuch.*

for protection when loading and emptying the kiln. Some potters use heat-resistant Kevlar mitts to lift large pots at red heat from the kiln. This could be extremely dangerous – one slip can mean disaster. As an alternative, I suggest devising a system whereby the pots are reduced without being moved from where they have been fired; there are several kiln designs in this book which could form a basis for your needs.

A pyrometer offers a useful guide to the temperature inside the kiln, but most raku potters fire by eye and never use a pyrometer. I have found one useful when demonstrating as it tells me when to pay attention to the kiln, not the audience.

Setting up for firing

Choose the site for your firing with care. It should be an open area, away from buildings, away from anything which might catch fire, and clear of people and pets. Allow yourself plenty of room for your activities. Make sure you have everything you need. A basic checklist will include:

- Kiln and fuel
- Matches or lighter
- Reduction chamber(s)
- Reduction material
- Water-filled container or spray for quenching, if required
- Tongs and gloves
- Work to be fired

- Hose and/or buckets of water for safety

Plan ahead – think of the movements you will be making during the firing. Make sure that when you take the lid off your kiln, you have somewhere safe, and fireproof, to put it. The space between the kiln and the reduction chamber needs to be completely clear of obstructions. Note particularly the hose from the propane cylinder. The reduction materials should be stored a safe distance from any flame.

It is good practice to try out cold everything you will be doing – literally. This way you should either know everything is in place, or have adequate time to make adjustments before the real heat of the moment makes this difficult. And no matter how many raku firings you do, *never* get complacent.

Reduction materials

After your work has been fired it will be reduced in a container of some kind using combustible materials. After firing, most raku work is treated to a second trial by fire in that it is placed in sawdust, newspaper or other combustibles. This is usually referred to as either reduction or carbonisation.

Reduction means reducing the amount of oxygen in the atmosphere surrounding your pots. We can acheive this inside the kiln by restricting the flow of gases – partially covering the flue with a piece of ceramic fibre board will do this. The flame, hungry to burn, will take oxygen atoms from anything inside the kiln, and in doing so can change the colour of both the clay and glaze. Raku

Bob Smith with his work inside a reduction bin, and straw used for reducing.

potters who favour copper reds frequently do this for the last few minutes of a firing.

However, most raku is reduced immediately after the pots have been taken from the kiln by placing them in an enclosed container with something that will burn (for example, sawdust). The combustibles burst into flames, taking oxygen atoms from the clay and glaze and thus changing the work in the process. Carbon produced during reduction penetrates the exposed clay body, and the craze lines in the glaze, turning the body to grey and black. I have used the term reduction when referring to this process throughout the book.

It is certainly worth experimenting with different reduction substances – what you use will contribute to the individuality of your work, and will partly depend on what is available locally. I have heard of combustibles as diverse as coffee grounds and banana leaves being used.

Sawdust is most commonly used for reduction, so straight away you have the choice of new or seasoned, hardwood and softwood, mixed or single species. Some potters will only use a specific kind of sawdust, others are happy to accept a random mix. Wood shavings will tend to give a less dense crazing which you may prefer.

Rob Sollis uses equestrian bedding, which consists of very fine flakes of wood, somewhere between sawdust and wood shavings. A large bale costs around £6 (US$9). He reduces his glazed pieces first, only using it for his black-ware when it has become well charred.

Andrew Mason, who fires to 1080°C (1976°F), quite high for raku, uses densely packed straw in a metal bin to give heavy reduction and provide some protection from thermal shock.

Bob Smith primarily uses bone-dry straw or field grass. He writes: *This is quite smoky, but the straw marks (or ash resist marks from the burnt straw) are quite attractive, giving a random, reed-like, truly raku flavour.* In addition, he occasionally uses sawdust, leaves, or shredded newspaper.

Rick Hirsch uses hay or straw or sawdust 'depending on the kind of marks I want to leave'.

Susan Luker uses oak shavings for her resist-slip pieces. She writes: *If I use softwoods such as pine, the pine sweats, and can condense into water droplets which sometimes penetrate the slip/glaze layer and leave an unseemly brown tar mark.*

Some potters prefer to reduce with newspaper. Kristin Doner is one ; she fires indoors, in a room with a 15ft (4.5 m) high ceiling – and a fire sprinkler directly above the kiln which has never yet been set off! She lifts the body of the kiln off the pot, and places two sheets of newspaper rolled up into a log into the hot firebox, which sets the paper alight. The reduction container is then placed over the work. She writes: *Most people think you need a ton of newspaper and smoke to achieve reduction; you don't. The most newspaper I've ever used is four sheets, and I decided even that was overkill.* (I don't think the political perspective taken by a newspaper affects the artistic integrity of the pot in any way, but it may adversely influence your state of mind!) The reduction chamber is inverted over the (fired) work, with its rim sitting on a layer of sand which acts as a seal.

Note: Never use sawdust from any kind of composition board such as MDF. Firstly, the chemicals involved in its manufacture could damage your health. Secondly, your work may be left with a horrible aroma. I once used the

Kristin Doner, brush-stroked teapot, slip resist, h. 18 cm (7 in.). *Photograph by Kristin Doner.*

A few potters do not use a container but simply sprinkle sawdust on their work to give localised reduction, perhaps freezing this with a light spray of water.

First firing

Once the firing site is set up to your satisfaction, you can start the kiln. If you are using propane as your fuel, point the burner away from you when you light it, and *don't* turn the gas full on. The burner nozzle should be placed about 2.5 cm (1 in.) away from the firemouth – too close or inside the firemouth and you will melt the front of the burner, too far away and insufficient heat will go into the kiln. The burner should be secured in place with a fixed metal bracket or a heavy brick.

The pots to go into any firing must be dry. If not, they will explode from the internal pressure of steam trying to escape. If you are glazing on the same day as the firing, dry your work on top of a hot kiln, or even in a warm oven.

When placing your work in the kiln, don't pack too tightly. You need to allow plenty of room for lifting the pots from the kiln. One false move with the tongs and pots can touch, which means they either stick together, or the molten glaze forms strings between them. Some pieces, eg. vases, can be lifted vertically, but a shallow bowl is likely to tilt when grabbed with the tongs, and you need to make allowances for the resulting movement.

Fire on a low flame for the first part of the firing (to around 150°C/300°F) in order to let the steam escape. After that, gradually turn up the gas to achieve a steady temperature rise. Too much gas and the temperature in the firing chamber can be uneven. If the fuel cannot burn properly, and you see flames coming from the flue, the

sweepings from under the circular saw in a school, and, although I washed the pots after firing, and even soaked them in various detergents for days, I never got rid of the vile smell.

Reduction chamber

For the post-firing reduction you need a container of some kind, one which can be sealed with a lid, or inverted on a sand or sawdust bed. Whatever you use needs to be fireproof – plastic is out!

Most potters use a galvanised metal waste bin for reduction – it's inexpensive, comes with a close-fitting metal lid, and is a convenient size. For smaller pieces I use a metal bucket, sealing the rim with a kiln shelf. John Wheeldon reduces his pieces one at a time under inverted catering-size food tins, though for demonstrations he uses an inverted galvanised pan over three or four pots.

temperature may even fall back.

As the kiln approaches temperature you will see the glaze start to melt and bubble. It is when this bubbling settles that you have to start thinking about taking the pots from the kiln. There are three ways of ascertaining glaze maturity:

1. By eye – does the glaze look smooth, and without any blemishes?
2. Shining a torch onto the surface of a pot is a surprisingly effective way of examining the glaze surface.
3. Holding a metal rod near the pot and checking its reflection in the glaze – a method used by Lynda Harris in New Zealand.

Once you are happy with the glaze melt, it is time to remove your work from the kiln. Have the tongs ready, **turn off the gas**, and open the kiln.

Subsequent firings

Because the kiln has already been heated, and stays relatively hot despite being opened, subsequent firings will be much quicker than the first of the day. Depending on the design of your kiln, the shelf may remain very hot – this is especially true of top-loaders – and may crack the base of cold pots when they are placed in the kiln. To avoid this, place your work on a biscuit tile, on clay buttons, or on ceramic fibre pads – anything which will form a barrier between the hot shelf and your work.

Be very careful putting work into a hot kiln – wear protective gloves, and clothing with sleeves.

Tim Andrews checking resist-slip on 'Humbug' in the kiln. *Photograph by Tim Andrews.*

Above Tim Andrews carrying a hot pot to the reduction chamber.
Below left Tim Andrews reducing in a waste bin.
Below right 'Humbug' after firing, with partly shelled resist slip.

Tim Andrews removing resist-slip layer from a pot. *Photograph by Sandra Andrews.*

Variations on firing techniques

In-kiln reduction

To achieve a good copper glaze, some potters reduce in the kiln for a few minutes at the end of the firing. This can be achieved by:

1. Increasing the amount of gas going into the kiln until a flame shows at the flue.
2. Partially closing the flue with a piece of ceramic fibre or kiln brick; again, you should see a small flame at the flue. (Lead glazes react instantly and badly to reduction, producing bubbles and blisters; other glazes are unaffected in this way.)

Tony White, placing ducks in the reduction chamber.

Firing with an electric kiln

Because of the heat retained by the brickwork in an electric kiln you will need additional protective clothing – thermal gloves for opening, protective face mask and goggles. Remember that an automatic cut-off is **vital** if you are firing with electricity.

Post-firing reduction

You do not need to rush your work from the kiln to the reduction chamber. Allow the glaze to cool slightly before lifting your pots from the kiln – I wait until I can hear the glaze pinging as the crazing begins to form. Molten glaze can stick to the tongs, though the marks made by them on the soft but no longer sticky glaze can be an added feature – an 'incidental' happening. However, placing the work in sawdust or wood shavings too soon can leave an unpleasantly rough, pitted surface.

When the glaze has 'set' sufficiently for the pot to be moved, it should be placed in the reduction container, which will already have a layer of sawdust or shavings at the bottom before receiving the first pot. Once in the bin, the pot needs to be covered with the reduction material, partly to achieve maximum effects, partly to prevent damage from being knocked by other pieces in the same container. If you need a better seal for the lid, layers of damp newspaper can be used, or a piece of ceramic fibre blanket. Remember that when you come to lift the lid of the reduction bin there will be tar created by smoke and water vapour residues on the underside which can drip and stain clothing permanently.

Quenching

To quench or not to quench? Some potters never quench (except in demon-stration situations), preferring to allow their work to cool naturally, so avoiding any unnecessary thermal shock. Others use quenching creatively to freeze reduction effects, either spraying specific areas, or dunking the whole piece in water. Bob Smith (referring to his copper glaze), uses sparse reduction material on a bed of sand under a garbage bin. He writes: *If I reduce heavily, but don't leave the pot in reduction more than 15 minutes or so, and then quench with water very quickly, I get some reduced areas, some oxidised areas, and the inter-face between the two can include a rainbow/ oil slick range of colours. This is probably my favourite result with the copper glazes I use.*

Quenching a bottle form in water can be dangerous, as the water which collects inside can boil and then shoot out violently. If you have to quench a bottle, do not submerge it below the

neck, or else point it away from you – but not at anyone else!

Firing copper-matt pieces

Because of the difficulties in cleaning the velvet surface of these glazes, it is necessary to avoid any contamination of the glazed surface of the pot. After firing, John Wheeldon inverts the hot pot onto a bed of sawdust, and allows the resulting flames and hot gases to play on the pot. During this period he sprinkles sawdust lightly on the pot, both to keep the flame going and to create specific areas of reduction. After two minutes he places a catering size tin can over the pot, with more sawdust as the seal. (In demonstration situations he

Left John Wheeldon placing pots from the kiln upside-down on a bed of sawdust.
Above Pots in burning sawdust prior to being covered under a galvanised container.
Below The finished pots. Demonstration firing by John Wheeldon at the National Pottery and Ceramics Festival, Hatfield House. *Photographs by John Mathieson.*

uses a much larger galvanised metal container and reduces four pots at a time). The work is allowed to cool naturally. I should point out that John usually leaves the rims of his pieces unglazed, partly for artistic reasons as he enjoys the visual play between the matt black clay and the often spectacular colours of the glaze, and partly to avoid glaze contamination from the tars in the sawdust. He will sometimes use a small blowtorch in a manner rather like a brush to slightly alter the colours after the pot has cooled.

An alternative to John's reduction method would be to place the pot on a stand inside the reduction container so that it makes no direct contact with the reduction material. Newspaper, which does not contain tars, could be used as the fuel. As copper-matt effects are dependent on oxygen variations in the atmosphere immediately surrounding the pots, it will be necessary to lift the lid of the reduction chamber at intervals.

Firing with resist slips

Pots with resist slip are fired and reduced in the same way as any other glaze. After cooling comes the magical process of removing the slip-glaze layer, for which you should wear safety glasses. If you find the slip-glaze layer is sticking to the pot, try firing to a lower temperature, or use a clay with a higher vitrification temperature for the slip layer. You may be able to remove some imperfections with different grades of carborundum (wet and dry) paper – the finest grades will give a very smooth surface.

Firing crackle glazes

Bob Smith cites a variety of factors which affect the crazing of the glaze.

He writes: *With the white crackle glaze, I can achieve several variations of crackle depending on; thickness of the glaze, thickness of the pot, length of time between the kiln and reduction, length of time in reduction, selectively applied air or water (or snow) before placing in the reduction barrel.*

Horst Kerstan selectively sprays water on his work to produce a line of very fine crackle against a background of more open crazing. With my own glaze the crazing is less bold and perhaps more delicate if the work is reduced on sawdust under a tin can.

Fuming with soluble salts

While your work is still red-hot it can be sprayed with soluble salts. **These are dangerous chemicals and it is IMPERATIVE that you wear the appropriate face mask. Do not get the materials on your skin or clothing.**

Bob Smith writes of ferric chloride: *This is a very serious ingredient, and potentially very dangerous. The effects on the pot, however, can be stunning, giving a reddish to rust to amber to honey colour, depending on application. A relatively short reduction time of five to eight minutes, and quick quenching, can result in some beautiful black reduction marks.*

Refiring

There are potters who routinely refire their work a number of times until they are satisfied with the result. Some clays are very forgiving and will allow you to do this, while others will not tolerate the repeated stress involved. It really is a case of try it and see – but try it with an insignificant piece of work rather than with something precious.

After firing

When firing with propane, remember to turn off both the burner *and* the bottle when you finish. If you forget, a dangerous amount of propane can escape from the bottle as you disconnect the burner.

Cleaning your work

After reduction in sawdust or wood shavings, tars will have formed on the surface of your pot, sometimes giving the appearance of a lustre. Potters have spent endless hours researching the best way to get rid of this residue, and all of their findings involve hard scrubbing of some kind. My own technique is to use water with washing-up liquid, a suede brush (which consists of fine brass wire bristles) and 'Spontex' scouring pads. These pads appear to be made from stainless steel swarf (metal turnings from a lathe), and unlike steel wool do not rust and disintegrate. I have found that soaking pieces in water and washing powder for several days makes removing the residue from the inside of bottles (using a stiff paintbrush) an easy task.

David Jones uses wire wool, abrasive papers, and diamond pads to produce a very fine, smooth surface. Rick Foris uses a soft nylon dish scrubber with a mild cleanser. David Atamanchuk uses water and a steel brush. Nesrin During uses a household sponge and Vim (a coarse domestic scouring powder). And Kristin Doner never needs to clean her work.

For his blackware – which cannot be scrubbed in the normal way after firing – Rob Sollis uses pre-burnt and therefore tar-free equestrian bedding when reducing. The blackware emerges smooth from the reduction; any small tar residues can be removed with a fine

Gail Bakutis reducing, Rufford Ceramic Centre. *Photograph by John Mathieson.*

abrasive slip which he rubs over the wet pot with his hand. Rob does not wax his pots as he prefers to see the natural clay surface.

Wear rubber gloves when cleaning your work. I know from experience that some domestic chemicals are far from kind to your hands.

Rob Sollis removing a large 'atom' form from the reduction chamber.
Right Rob Sollis cleaning 'atom' form with a fine abrasive slip. *Photographs by Alun Tipping.*

Waxing

Some potters polish their unglazed pieces with beeswax or furniture polish. This can give colours an extra 'lift', especially when the work has been burnished. Once a piece has been waxed, this needs to be repeated every year or so. If you practice this technique, use a quality product.

Cleaning up

Whether it's my own place, or an educational establishment, I have always liked to leave studios reasonably clean and tidy after I finish work. The same goes for the firing area. Clear up when you finish. In particular, store unused chemicals and combustibles safely, and dispose of any broken pots carefully. If your kiln is a permanent structure, block any holes which might be attractive to small creatures. If you have any concerns or problems regarding the safe disposal of materials, contact your local environment protection agency for advice. I think everyone on the planet should be aware of their environmental responsibilities and take as much care as possible of their small part of the world.

Chapter Ten
Makers' Profiles

Kristin Doner (USA)

Kristin lives and works in Oakland, California. Her work has appeared in *Ceramics Monthly*, and she was recently given First Place in ceramics by her peers at the Sausalito Arts Festival, regarded as one of the most prestigious shows in the USA.

After highschool, Kristin studied ceramics for a short time in Washington DC, and later returned to clay 'for de-stressing while working in the high-tech world'. The courses and workshops she attended focused mainly on handbuilding and raku. Eventually she left her job to concentrate on ceramics.

Kristin views the raku process 'as a journey, in and of itself – raku lends itself well to the exploration inherent in the production of artwork'. The process is the focus for her, rather than the final result; therefore, the process itself is an inspiration. This can involve explorations with chemicals and fire, and with trying to repeat fascinating 'mistakes'. Other influences on her work include ancient history, the forms and textures on artifacts, primitive ways of making pottery, and primitive tools.

Kristin makes handbuilt vessels, mainly standing on tripods, with necks and stoppers, lids, handles and spouts. Some of the lids are bound to the vessel with cord, which brings a sense of mystery and underscores the ritual aspect of the work. She writes: *When an archaeologist finds a vessel, it is something to be examined and speculated about. It's the same sense of intense interest that I'm trying to create with my vessels.*

Kristin usually starts with a pinchpot formed from a large block of clay. This is

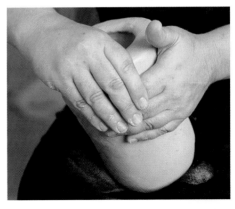

Kristin Doner, opening out 3.5 kg (8 lb) ball of clay using the pinchpot method; and beginning shaping with a paddle.
Photographs by James Dawson.

shaped by hand and with a paddle to form the body of the piece; initially the pot is held in the hand, though later in the forming process it is supported in a padded bowl. She sometimes uses slabs in combination with this technique. (There are similarities between this method and some traditional African and Asian ways of making pots.) When the pot is firm enough lugs, legs, spouts and other features are added. She uses terra sigillata quite often, especially with 'naked raku' (see sacrificial glazing, p.26), spraying one layer onto greenware, and up to three further thin layers on biscuit-ware. The completed work is biscuit fired to cone 010 (900°C/1652°F) in an electric kiln with a kilnsitter/programmer.

Left and below left Shaping base of pot; shaping shoulder of pot. *Photographs by James Dawson.*
Below Red and black amphora 28 cm x 26.5 cm (11 in. x 10.5 in.). Colour from red terra sigillata. *Photograph by MaxImage, San Francisco.*

Kristin Doner, bottles, 'unearthed' glaze, height: 25cm (10 in.). *Photograph by MaxImage, San Francisco, California.*

Kristin uses a lithium-based glaze which contributes to the feelings of time-lessness associated with her work, as the variegated surfaces she achieves gives her pieces a, literally, unearthed appearance, reflecting her interest in ancient history and artefacts.

She will also occasionally apply a sulphate solution to the red-hot pot as it emerges from the kiln. 'This is any colour-giving sulphate mixed with water. I never measure'.

Clay used:
• Standard raku body with 25% grog and 25% ball clay (the remainder being mostly kaolin).

Rob Sollis (UK)

After discovering clay whilst still at school – and frequently cycling home with a 25 kg (55 lb) bag of clay slung across the handlebars of his bike – Rob trained for four years as a production thrower at Dartington Pottery, Devon. The pottery on the Dartington estate had been founded by Bernard Leach in 1932, while the Dartington Pottery Training Workshop was established in 1975. At the time of Rob's arrival Janice Tchalenko, Harrow trained, and a tutor at the Royal College of Art, was employed as designer, and was replacing the orientally-inspired wares with pots of a more European shape and colour. Being involved in these changes had a great impact on Rob, and he still maintains strong links with Dartington.

A chance meeting with the Norwegian potter Geir Jensen led to more than ten years production throwing, initially in Norway and later in the UK. Rob established his own workshop in early 18th-century barns at Fishacre Mill, Littlehempston, only a couple of miles from Dartington. He exported biscuit-ware to Norway and began experiment-ing with raku, using the same clay he used for the Norwegian range, a smooth body rich in Molochite and high-alumina ball clay.

Rob produces two related bodies of work in raku – crackle-glazed pieces, some with burnished rims; and burnished forms, unglazed on the exterior, which are blackened in the sawdust post-firing. His concerns are with form and surface; he allows the glaze and the burnished surface to complement the shape, but does not add further decoration. All his work is thrown on the wheel, with some very tall pieces being made in two sections.

After turning, a steel kidney is used for burnishing where this is required, followed a day later by burnishing with the palm of the hand as the pot turns on the wheel. The rounded forms with very small bases are held in a chuck during this process, with a cloth to protect the surface. Rob tells me he can see the reflection of his fingertips in the resulting satin-smooth surface. All work is subsequently biscuit fired to 970°C (1778°F) in a 17 cu. ft (0.5 m³) electric kiln overnight on Economy Seven (the

Left to right from top Rob Sollis' workshop. Rob Sollis throwing large 'atom' form; turning inverted pot; burnishing 'atom' form; final hand-burnishing of inverted 'atom'. *Photographs by Alun Tipping.*

66

Rob Sollis, two large 'atom' forms. *Photograph by Alun Tipping.*

off-peak, cheaper UK electricity option).

For his glazed pieces, Rob uses crackle white, pale blue, and pale and deep green, all based on the same recipe. Work is glazed by dipping or pouring, often with part of the body left exposed, as Rob likes the dramatic contrast of the burnished black of the clay with the crackle glaze.

On his other body of work Rob glazes only the inside of his pieces, often with a copper glaze. This allows the outside of the pot – satin-matt to the touch, from the burnishing of the fine clay he uses – to accept the gifts of the post-firing reduction process, leaving a tracery of delicate markings on a charcoal grey ground.

Clay used:
• Equal parts of Molochite 200s mesh and TWVD Ball Clay

Tim Andrews (UK)

Tim trained with David Leach and at Dartington Pottery before setting up his own workshop. He now lives in Woodbury, not far from Exeter, where, besides his studio, he runs a gallery featuring a number of prominent makers. His own work has been widely exhibited internationally, and he is the author of *Raku – a Review of Contemporary Work*, and of the video *Tim Andrews – Raku and Smoke-fired Ceramics*.

Tim's interest in raku began early – in the engaging preface to his book he writes of celebrating his 18th birthday (coming-of-age in the UK) with a raku party. However, he made domestic ware and individual pieces in both stoneware and porcelain for a number of years, something he still does for long-standing customers. The decision to concentrate on raku stemmed partly from the realisation that, rather than being a

67

potter, he was essentially a creator of surfaces for on-glaze decoration. At present, his work is becoming larger and more sculptural, but is always related to a vessel of some sort.

Tim uses a fine crackle glaze, and a copper-matt (which he sprays onto the pot), but the bulk of his work employs resist slip, often over a coloured, burnished slip. Some pots, perhaps with wax resist markings, are simply dipped in the resist slip and then the glaze; he blows air into the glaze to trap bubbles, which result in random black dots on the finished pieces. On other works he builds up patterns using masking tape, which, after dipping in resist slip and glaze, is carefully removed. The edges of the patterns are meticulously cleaned – if there is glaze left on the surface of the pot it will leave a mark. The areas masked by the tape will be black after the raku firing. Yet another approach is to etch through the slip/glaze layer to reveal the clay body; again, these lines will be black after the firing. Using this variety of techniques Tim has produced a cohesive and immediately recognisable body of work.

Tim biscuit fires his work in a homebuilt front-loading gas kiln to 1030°–1050°C (1886°–1922°F), 'depending upon how much burnish I am prepared to lose. The porcelain content (of the body) allows for a higher biscuit temperature which I like in order to give the pieces some strength.'

Clays used:
• Roughly equal parts of T-material and Potclays Harry Fraser 1149 porcelain; more T-material is used for larger pieces – 'maybe 65:35 – I don't measure it'.
• Sometimes Y-material is substituted for T-material, with a higher proportion being used.

Tim Andrews, 'Humbug', diameter: 30 cm (12 in.). *Photograph by Sam Bailey.*

Tim Andrews, gourd forms, resist slip. *Photograph by Sam Bailey.*

Susan Luker (UK)

After a varied career, Susan took an art and design course at Plymouth College of Art and Design, where she was introduced to clay; after seeing the end of year ceramics show, and going to a Saturday raku workshop, she was hooked. With very little technical tutoring available at the college she read books and magazine articles, and talked to other potters. The workshop she used as a student – a stone barn on a working farm – is where the raku firings now take place, with the pots being made in a large shed at her home a mile away.

Susan's inspiration comes from nature. A profusion of red berries seen

Susan Luker, 'Oxalis'.

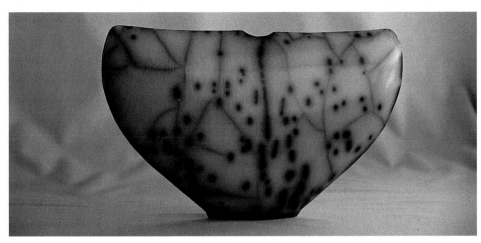

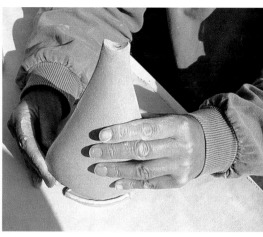

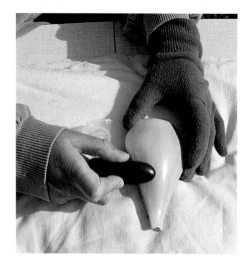

Left to right from top
Susan Luker, cutting 'teardrop' shape using a
paper template; applying de-grogged slip to
the edges to be joined; bringing the two
halves of the pot together; adding the base;
burnishing the slip with a polished stone.

against a bare hedge in winter inspired
the use of small contrasting markings
of red glaze. The smoke markings are
reminiscent of tree branches seen
against a winter sky. The sunset, reflected
along the winding marshland by the
River Avon, inspired her rivers of glaze.
The surface of her pots is representa-
tional of water-worn pebbles.

70

Susan Luker, vases.

Susan works with slabs of clay, rolled out with guides – small pots are 0.5 cm (³⁄₁₆ in.) thick, larger ones 1 cm (⅜ in.). She uses a template to cut the two sides of each piece. These are allowed to dry a little on plaster batts before being gently shaped by pushing with a rubber kidney to a hollow boat shape. Wanting each piece to be individual, Susan does not use plaster moulds or formers, but holds the work in her hand or on her arm. When she is satisfied that both sides are equal, they are joined using a de-grogged slip, and the base is added.

Susan paints a burnishing slip on all her work, consisting of equal parts of body clay (sieved 200s mesh) and porcelain. She writes: 'catching the slip at the right dryness to burnish is an art in itself. Burnish too soon and ripples appear in the clay body, too late and start/stop marks happen.' She uses a pebble to burnish, and holds the pot in a cotton-gloved hand to avoid leaving fingermarks. For the final burnish Susan uses a clean polythene bag wrapped over her finger to give a good shine. The work is biscuit fired to 1010°C (1850°F) in an electric kiln.

Some of Susan's work involves the use of latex masking before pouring the resist slip over the pot. The latex is peeled away, allowing direct painting of glazes onto the pot surface. Combining these techniques allows her to create her rivers of glaze across the burnished surfaces of her pieces.

Clays used:
• Valentine Earthstone Handbuilding (ES40) for larger pieces, and Earthstone Original (ES5) for smaller work.

Bob Smith (USA)

After military service Bob decided, out of conviction, that he wanted to become a teacher. In graduate school, while studying for teaching credentials, he 'discovered clay, fell in love with it, and changed all directions at that point'. He found a flier advertising a clay workshop in Colorado, decided to go, and encountered Paul Soldner, one of the major American raku artists. Soldner made a great impression on him: 'I loved the freedom, spontaneity of process, the lifestyle, of this one artist'. However, Bob was convinced that there was no money in this form of decorative art, and applied himself to becoming a stoneware and porcelain potter, doing raku for roughly one month a year. His interest and involvement increased until, by 1976, he was making exclusively raku. He writes: *I loved the immediacy of the process, the attention to the individual piece of art, and the pace, which seemed to me to be less frantic, less repetitive, than making domestic ware (which to this day I still love, buy, and regularly use).*

Bob cites as initial early influences Soldner's *joie de vivre*, and Peter Voulkos' 'organic manipulation of the medium', and latterly ancient Korean, Chinese, Japanese and Mediterranean work which he finds can be 'heady with a contemporary feel'. He says he seeks to make work based on the historical but which has something about it that makes it seem of the moment; 'not edgy or avant-garde or trendy, but new and contemporary – raku lends itself to this so well'.

Bob works in a converted south-facing, three-car garage next to his house. Here he has a large workspace with a wheel, tables, a slab roller and an extruder, plus an office, and a room for the electric kiln. The bulk of his work is

Bob Smith, five-piece wall panel, each 45 cm x 15 cm (18 in. x 6 in.).

Bob Smith, 'Pot on Tray', 19 cm x 18 cm
(7½ in. x 7 in.).

vessel-oriented, with sculptural elements
added in the form of extruded attach-
ments and handles constructed from
slabs. Some pieces are placed on trays
or altars, with small feet, giving a ritual,
ceremonial feel. He also makes wall
pieces in five or more sections, and
employs stamps and areas of contrasting glaze to create repeating and oppos-
ing patterns, some quiet, some more
commanding.

Bob biscuit fires in a 25-year-old
8 cu. ft (0.23 m³) Skutt kiln to cone 06
(1000°C/1832°F), with the elements on
low for four hours, medium for two, and
on high for a further two hours.

Clays used:
• Bob has created his own clay which is
marketed by Mile Hi Ceramics, Denver,
Colorado as '2002 w/grog'.

Lynda Harris (NZ)

Lynda is self-taught, having learned to
make pots by trial and error, and by
attending weekend schools. She has
been a full-time potter since 1984,
making tableware and one-off raku
pieces. She has since studied at Monash
University in Australia.

Lynda lives amongst 10 acres (16 km)
of native bush at Karekare on the west
coast of Auckland, and uses the ideas
generated by this environment to
decorate both raku and tableware,
naming individual pieces after birds
and plants. She writes: *The graphic
elements have a very distinctive New
Zealand flavour, and the intensity of
the light and colours in our country
are reflected in the colours that are made
possible by using the raku technique.* She
adds: *Raku firing always creates new
challenges and though at times it can be a
difficult and frustrating medium to elect to*

73

use, the rewards are also great when all the elements combine successfully. That is the magic of raku.

Lynda's slab forms are built using board as a support – a form of press-moulding. The design and size of each of her pieces is pre-determined, with the moulds being cut from board to the required size. These are loosely nailed together, and the slabs of clay placed inside the mould and then joined using thick slip, with a coil being pressed into the seam. Lynda points out that 'the joins have to be very thoroughly made as this is one of the main points of weakness during raku firing', (see the image on p.14). Some lidded pieces begin life as enclosed forms, and these need a hole pierced to allow air to escape; if not, the seams can burst as the piece shrinks.

When the pot is dry enough to handle – usually the next day – a curved Surform blade is used to achieve a clean form, and the surface is smoothed with a metal kidney. At this stage cutting the lid for a box form can be done. Lynda biscuit fires to 1000°C (1832°F).

Lynda decorates her slab-built pieces using thin strips of masking tape to separate different areas of colour, which are then painted on. Stains are added to a white crackle base glaze to give the colours she requires. Her slab-built pieces incorporate New Zealand imagery such as native trees, flowers and birds.

Left Lynda Harris, slab-built boxes, 'Nikau', 'Pururi' and 'Karake'.
Below 'Nikau' slab bowl.

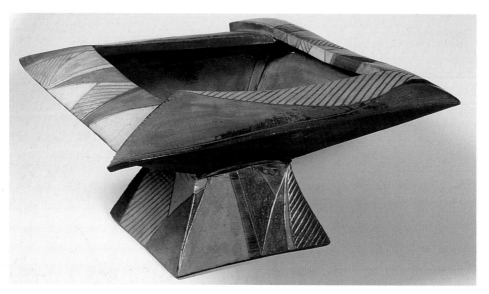

Rick Foris (USA)

Rick Foris' first exposure to clay was at the University of Wisconsin in the early 1970s, where he went on to major in ceramics. Most of his independent study at university was in raku: 'I loved the immediacy of the firing process, and was captivated by the lustrous surfaces of the glaze. Also I'm quite a low-tech type of person and the whole raku process certainly can fit into that category.' After graduating, he formed a co-operative pottery studio with five other potters and worked in functional stoneware, salt-glaze, and raku. Since 1979 he has concentrated entirely on raku, making works that are basically non-functional sculptural vessels.

Rick does not use ceramics as the source of his inspiration. In fact, he will deliberately go out of his way to avoid looking at contemporary ceramics in magazines and galleries. He is most influenced by architectural details such as 'stairways, courtyards, stelae'. Language also interests him: 'I incorporate slip-trailed and impressed characters into many of my pieces. Not actual languages – just shapes I make up that suggest language – pyroglyphs'. In his artist's statement he writes: *My work reflects many influences, though none consciously. This maintains an element of mystery in both the shapes of the vessels and the impact of the surface. My designs suggest other cultures and languages but are purely of my own fabrication. This leaves my work open to interpretation by the viewers, who see what they want to see rather than what I want them to see. The combination of traditional raku firing with the brilliance of acrylic paint melds a sense of timelessness with contemporary thought.*

Rick's studio is in a 24 ft x 36 ft (7.2 m x 10.8 m) building beside his home. The main room is 24 ft x 24ft (7.2 m x 7.2 m), and contains a wheel, slab roller, de-airing pugmill, spray booth, work tables and shelves. The electric kiln is in a smaller room, with the raku kiln located outside on a concrete slab.

Work is generally wheel-thrown to start with, and usually incorporates handbuilt elements such as handles and spouts. Rick also builds multi-component slab bases; these are fired separately and joined together later with epoxy resin.

Rick Foris, vessel (finished with acrylics), 36 cm x 30 cm x 56 cm (14 in. x 12 in. x 22 in.) *Photograph by Bill Lemke.*

Rick Foris, vessel (finished with acrylics), 30 cm x 30 cm x 43 cm (12 in. x 12 in. x 17 in.)
Photograph by Bill Lemke.

This enables him to ensure each section dries completely flat, and to vary the degree of smoking of the different parts through black to grey and white.

Because of the number of slab bases Rick makes, he biscuit fires slowly, starting the kiln early in the morning and easing it up slowly during the day. The total time elapsed is usually 12 hours. He uses a 10 cu. ft (0.3 m³) electric kiln and fires to cone 08 (950°C/1742°F).

Clays used:

This body, Rick's own recipe used by him for the last 20 years, is made for him by the Paoli Clay Co. Paoli, Wisconsin. Rick tells me that many US potters also include Kyanite in their clay body 'for increased fired strength and thermal-shockability'.

Gold Art Clay   600 (37.25%)
A.P.Green Fireclay   400 (24.85%)
Ball clay (OM4)   250 (15.5%)
Grog   275 (17.1%)
Feldspar (Custer)   85 (5.3%)

Gertrud Båge and Lena Andersson (SW)

Gertrud and Lena have worked together since 1984, firing at Lena's workshop in Karsjo, four hours north of Stockholm. Gertrud writes: 'I have my workshop in central Stockholm and must leave the city to do the glaze firing. A couple of times a year I pack a car full of biscuit pots and travel to Lena. We concentrate on firing for five days.'

The ceramic fibre kilns are situated in a spacious workshop with wide doors leading to the reduction containers outdoors. 'Only strong winds stop us firing as there are quite a few trees nearby. We have fired in February when we drop the warm reduced pots straight into the snow.'.

Gertrud uses the wheel to make plates, bowls and vases, and slabs for boxes, dishes and tiles. For larger pieces

Gertrud Båge, plate, diameter: 29 cm (11½ in.).

Gertrud Båge, square dish, width: 38 cm (15 in.).
Right Lena Andersson, starfish.
Below Lena Andersson, tiled wall.

she uses T-material, and for smaller shapes K129 from Vingerling. She has found a Swedish clay, Fyle, that works for raku if grog is added. She biscuit fires the K129 to 1060°C (1940°F), and the T-material to 1000°C (1832°F), in an electric kiln.

Lena handbuilds, making small sculptural pieces, tiles for kitchens and bathrooms, and large wall decorations for both private and public places. Her wall and column tiling often involve complex geometrical patterns. She also makes iridescent insects, sometimes in multiples forming wall decorations. She biscuit fires to 1000°C (1832°F).

Jim Bassett (UK)

Jim has had a long involvement with clay and was Senior Lecturer in Ceramics at University College, Northampton, for many years. He has worked in a variety of different ways but is perhaps best known for his slip-decorated earthenware dishes commemorating events such as birth and marriage. Working in raku, he devised a series of press-moulded insects up to 12 cm (4¾ in.) long which look particularly effective grouped on a wall or tree-trunk. Many is the unsuspecting guest who has returned terrified from the privy late of an evening.

The variety of effects that can be achieved by overpainting a transparent base glaze with different colours is amazing. Audiences are captivated as these almost iridescent colours emerge from beneath the blackened sawdust after a firing.

Once the prototype has been made in clay, and the plaster mould(s) cast from this, clay is simply pressed into the mould and allowed to dry slightly before being removed. When the clay is leatherhard, the edge is trimmed and two holes pierced at the eyes. This allows a loop of nichrome wire to be inserted to enable the bug to be lifted from the kiln. Later two nails can be hammered through to hold the insect on a wall, and to form the antennae.

Jim biscuit fires to 1020°C (1868°F) in an electric kiln.

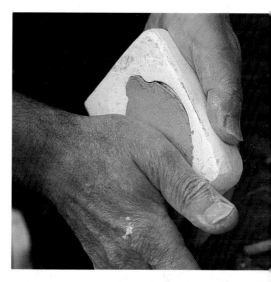

Below Bug press-moulds made by Jim Bassett. *Photograph by John Mathieson.*
Right Jim Bassett, pressing clay into plaster mould; bug removed from mould. *Photographs by John Mathieson.*

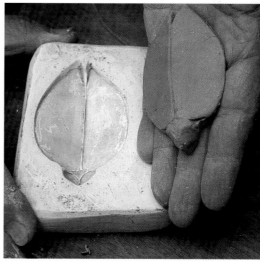

Jim Bassett, bugs. *Photograph by John Mathieson.*

David Jones (UK)

David Jones graduated in philosophy and literature from Warwick University. Whilst there he met an American exchange student who, deciding the university would not be complete without a pottery, applied for, and received, funding to establish a studio. David took over the running of the facility some six months later, and has followed a career in ceramics ever since. His fascination with raku began after reading Bernard Leach's account in *A Potter's Book*, and Paul Soldner's description of his reinterpretation of the technique. He is currently senior lecturer in the ceramics department of the University of Wolverhampton. He took part in the major British raku

David Jones, three vessels 'Crackled Skin', height (tallest): 38 cm (15 in.).

David Jones, double-walled vessel 'Dark Noise', 20 cm x 9 cm (8 in. x 3 ½ in.).

exhibition at the Rufford Ceramics Centre in 1985. Following the publication of his book *Raku – investigations into fire*, he was co-curator of the exhibition of the same name at Rufford in 2000, a speaker and exhibitor at the International Raku Symposium in Korea 2001, and organiser of the Raku Symposium held at Rufford the same year.

Concerning working in raku, David writes: *I must cite the excitement of the process and particularly the intimate relationship between potter and pot continuing into the firing. It thus also becomes the interplay of kiln and artist – the sense of involvement with the work is thus a more profound one than leaving the pot at the 'church door' of an electric kiln.*

Most of David's work is thrown and altered, with handbuilt additions. He writes: *The work takes as its influences the vessels of the Japanese Tea ceremony – in particular the tea bowl. This is further informed by my own take on the references of the Japanese masters – the impressions and markings of nature, from the erosion of a seaside rock pool, revisiting the concentric markings left by the abrasions of the sea, to the systematic dragging of a plough across the countryside.* He will freely mark the interior of bowls with rough tools, whilst giving the exterior a machined finish. Some of his vessels are double-walled; their surfaces are reminiscent of both landscapes, and of water moving around a stone in a stream.

David biscuit fires 'very slowly, and cautiously' to 980°C (1796°F) in an electric kiln.

After biscuit firing David decorates his work with graphic resist patterns using masking tape and latex resist. The pots are then sprayed with glazes, some incorporating precious metals including silver nitrate and gold chloride. Usually significant sections of his pots are left unglazed, resulting in a contrast between the blackened body and the colours of the glazed areas. He also fumes some work with stannous chloride post-firing.

Clays used:
• Valentine's Earthstone clays
• T-material and porcelain mixes

Rick Hirsch (USA)

Rick Hirsch's long and distinguished career in ceramics began on the art foundation course at the State University of New York, where he was required to take pottery. After studying for a Master's with Frans Wildenhain at the School of American Craftsmen, he taught at Boston University, and is now Professor at Rochester Institute of Technology, New York. He has been involved – as curator, juror, panel member, lecturer, writer, and exhibitor – in ceramic activities worldwide. With Christopher Tyler he is co-author of *Raku – Techniques for Contemporary Potters* (1975).

Rick's studio is called the 'Vessel Research Center'. It is a two-storey building with an outside kiln pad which

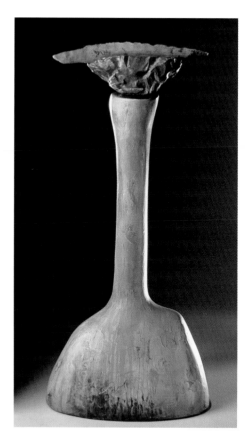

he constructed himself in a style sympathetic to his old farmhouse. He uses a variety of making techniques: 'I consider myself an 'assembler' in that I put parts together; within that I coil, slab, and throw, add and subtract.'

Of raku, Rick writes: *For me, raku is an attitude, a way of thinking and working. It is not a 'firing process' nor a 'technique'. My pieces are conceived as raku long before their introduction to fire. They are a reflection of what I think the definition of raku is. Raku captivates me. The variables are extensive, which makes individual*

Above Rick Hirsch, 'Pedestal Bowl # 16', height: 117 cm (46 in.).
Left Rick Hirsch, 'Primal Cup # 5', height: 29 cm (11½ in.).

*firings distinctive. Thus, each piece seizes
and reflects that specific period of action.
I do not make a separation between raku
and the content of my work. The fire
imprints achieved through the post-firing
are required pieces of information, vitally
contributing to the whole idea.*

The sources of his ideas – what Rick
refers to as 'the well spring' – are mainly
ancient artefacts. His tripod vessels are
'connected with and point directly
towards bronze ritual vessels from
Shang Dynasty China, along with
pre-Columbian earthenware tripod
containers'. However, his newer work
is much more eclectic, with 'sustenance
being drawn from multi-cultural archaic
ceremonial artefacts such as stone
basins, mortar and pestle, jade containers, tools and weaponry'. Some of his
latest pieces have been based on Chinese
Viewing Stones – natural objects placed
on special stands and displayed on a
writing desk for contemplation.

Since his work is very thick and
heavy, Rick biscuit fires slowly, over
three or four days, in an electric kiln
to between cone 08 and 06 (950°C/
1742°F and 1000°C/1832°F).

Clays used:

Rick mixes a clay body for throwing and
handbuilding:

White fireclay	35
White stoneware clay (mid-range)	25
Ball clay	15
Talc	10
Spodumene	5
Fine/medium grog	5 – 10

Tony and Barbara White (UK)

Tony originally trained in the manufac-
turing engineering industry, later learning about clay at evening classes. After
moving to Wales in 1983 he set up a
workshop making domestic stoneware
while working as the ceramics technician
at University College Wales at
Aberystwyth. It was here that a visiting
potter introduced him to raku. He writes:
*I was seduced by the firing and post-firing
process. There is a relationship between you
and the process, a bit like a human one,
some days good, others not so good.*

He established his present workshop
in rural mid-Wales in 1990. This is a
large, self-built wooden structure with
attached firing shed with a large extractor
fan. The workshop is equipped with a
pugmill, wheel, slab roller, electric kiln,
workbenches and a stove. Here he works
with his wife Barbara, Tony doing most
of the making and the firing, Barbara
most of the decorating. The majority of
their work consists of free-standing
animal and bird figures – cats (based on
their own), dogs, runner ducks, hens,
ravens, pigs – with some extruded forms
and thrown pieces. Some of the figures
are press-moulded, others slab-built and
cut to shape with the aid of templates.
As a direct contrast, Tony also likes to
experiment with semi-abstract decoration
on thrown pieces and extruded vases.
Surfaces to be left unglazed are burnished
before the biscuit firing, which is to
1000°C (1832°F) in a 4 cu. ft (0.11 m³)
electric kiln, with the kiln vented to
700°C (1292°F).

Clays used:

T-material

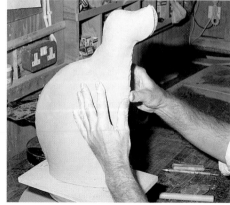
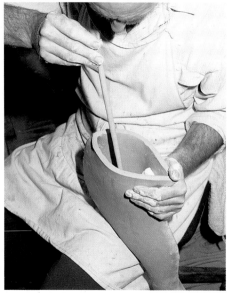

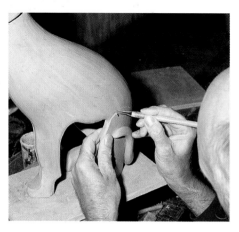

Left to right from top
Tony and Barbara White, using a template to
cut the sides of a dog; joining the sides of the
dog; reinforcing the join with a coil; adding
details to the head; adding details to the flank;
post-firing reduction of a dog in sawdust.

Above Tony and Barbara White, completed dog.
Below Cat and ducks. For both their animal and bird sculptures, and individual pieces, Tony and Barbara usually leave some (often large) areas burnished and without glaze. The low-temperature brush-on earthenware glazes they use are particularly appropriate to this approach, and provide a wide range of colours.
Right Slab-built vase.

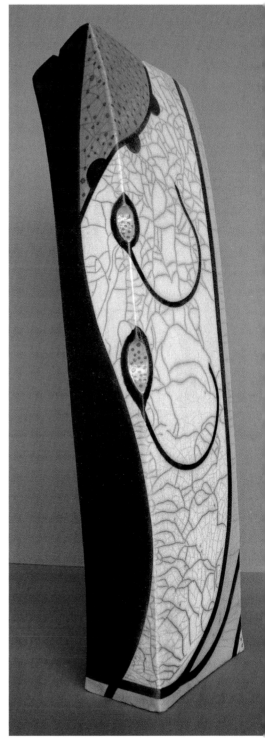

David Roberts (UK)

Through his work and his example, David Roberts has been enormously influential in the development of raku in the UK. His article in *Ceramic Review* in 1977 describing the construction of his ceramic fibre kiln was the first major introduction of this material to British readers. Further articles by and about him have enabled the readership to watch his growth as an artist, and to follow developments in the world of raku. He is one of the few British potters – and the only raku potter – to have a book devoted solely to his own work (see Bibliography). Until recently he was a lecturer on the Foundation Course at Dewsbury Art College in Yorkshire.

David's sparsely equipped studio is situated on the edge of Saddleworth Moor in West Yorkshire, in a countryside which has had a great influence on his work; some of his pieces appear to reference rock strata. All his work is built from extruded coils, which are added to a base created from a thumb-pot. His work is always vessel-related, though later pieces have become increasingly sculptural. He writes: *I am currently exploiting the way different strengths and patterns of carbonisation react to various surface treatments, so that surfaces can be burnished at the leatherhard stage, sanded when bone dry, or ground and polished, using wet and dry abrasive paper together with Diapads , both after the bisque and the final raku firing. Biscuit firing is to cone 06 (1000°C/1832°F) which gives a fairly strong body but which is open enough for the smoke to penetrate.*

Though David used glazes extensively in the early part of his career, he now favours the resist slip techniques previously described.

Clays used:
• Potclay's 1106 White St.Thomas plus 10% grog (20s mesh – dust)
• T-material 2:1 porcelain

David Roberts, 'Vessel with Lines', diameter: 34 cm (13½ in.), coil built, resist slip.

Ellen Rijsdorp and Jannie van der Wel (NL)

Jannie studied child welfare, education, and handicrafts and became a teacher, working with disabled children for many years. With her interest in the arts growing, she took a higher degree, where she had a particularly good ceramics teacher who encouraged her to work with clay. She subsequently taught crafts, later specialising in ceramics. She met Ellen Rijsdorp at the ceramic centre 'Kerade' in Delft, where they both teach; this led to the construction of a shared raku kiln. Of her work she writes:
Sometimes my work is related to man. Other work is dominated by architecture and nature. There is not one special person or style that influences me – it's a mixture from what I see, feel and think.

Jannie both throws and slab-builds, using different clays for each method. She refers to some of her thrown pieces as 'Japanese women'. Her buildings, constructed with the aid of a slab roller, remind me of the paintings of Giorgio de Chirico. She biscuit fires between 975° and 1025°C (1787° and 1877°F) for raku, naked raku, and copper-matt pieces. For terra sigillata she fires no higher than 950°C (1742°F).

Ellen Rijsdorp went to the Art Academy in Champion, but soon discovered that if she wanted to be 'a real potter' she had to go to the Ceramic School in Gouda, where she studied from 1984–91. During part of this time she spent six months of each year in Ghana, working on an ecological agricultural project, and being taught to make pots by the local women. Since 1990 she has taught with Jannie, and for a time was a demonstration thrower at the Delft Pottery.

Ellen now lives and has her studio in a

Left Jannie van der Wel, slab building under construction.
Below Jannie van der Wel, completed slab buildings.

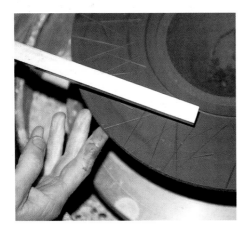

Left to right from top
Ellen Rijsdorp, throwing inverted disc form –
the centre remains open to form the bowl;
throwing inverted disc form – closing base of
central bowl; compressing the flange;
creating surface texture on the rim of the
central bowl; making indentations on the
flange. These will later sparkle with glaze.

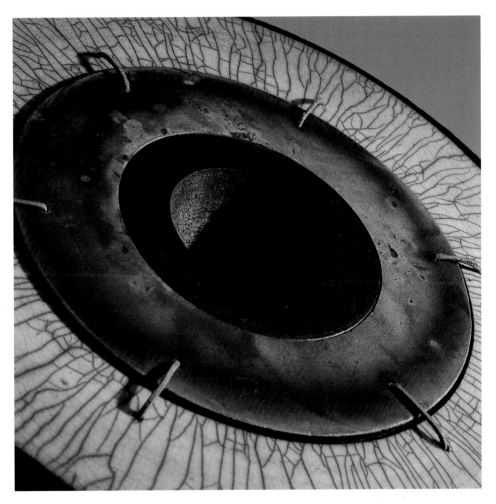

Ellen Rijsdorp, detail of disc form with resist slip and copper-matt glaze.

former gunpowder house built in 1660 (see website for more information: www.kruithuis.nl). After ceramic school she felt that although she was a competent production thrower, she knew little about her own artistic directions. *It took me a year to find out what I wanted to make. But now I know exactly how I want to work with clay. My shapes don't change radically but I make little steps. That's what I prefer.*

Jannie and Ellen use the same French KPLC Limoge Gres clay, with fine grog added; Jannie also uses Vigo Multi-pasta, which is similar to T-material. For resist slip Ellen uses mainly porcelain.

Ellen biscuit fires to 975°C (1787°F). If she uses a transparent glaze she refires in her biscuit kiln to 800°C (1472°F) prior to raku firing – she finds this method quicker than waiting for the glaze to melt in the raku kiln.

Nesrin During (NL)

Nesrin originally studied comparative literature at university; she is self-taught as a potter, and now teaches ceramics. She was drawn to raku through some wood-fired raku pieces she had seen, and it remains her central interest. Her method of constructing a wood-fired kiln is shown on pp.44–8. She has made functional pieces on the wheel, but now all her work is handbuilt with coils. In addition to raku she makes wood-fired stoneware.

Nesrin does not decorate her work. She writes: *Because my forms are most important, I am trying to perfect the form. And because I fire with wood, this makes the pieces very alive, different, interesting, unique – enough happens on the pot's surface.*
Clay used:
German Westervald clay with added sand, sometimes mixed with T-material for bigger pieces. The clay should be colour responsive because of the wood firing, and should contain some iron oxide.

Left Nesrin During, coiling.

Horst Kerstan (D)

Horst Kerstan has a long-established reputation for his wood-fired stoneware which he fires in a self-built anagama kiln. Since 1970 he has made numerous visits to Japan and Korea, and has absorbed many of the philosophies of the potters there. Attracted by the softer and warmer glazes, he began making raku in 1990.

Reflecting the Japanese influence on his life and work, Horst makes tea-ceremony vessels exclusively, and particularly likes producing tea bowls. He writes: *To me this is like a piano concerto, the virtuosity within the throwing process gives me the greatest pleasure. The liveliness of a tea bowl is of major significance to me. Thus, I re-discover Zen, and it is a touchstone for myself whether the receptacle has been a success or not.* He developed his own clay for his work, all of which is made on the wheel. He biscuit fires to the

Horst Kerstan, tea ceremony bowl.

91

relatively high temperature of 1100°C (2012°F).

Horst developed his own frit 'in order to be independent of the industry'. He uses white, yellow, green, salmon-red and apricot glazes, which he accents with gold chloride (red/pink and purple), silver chloride (yellow, and silver in heavy reduction), and copper nitrate (green).

Below Horst Kerstan, lidded jar.

Right Andrew Mason, vase with multi-coloured glazes.

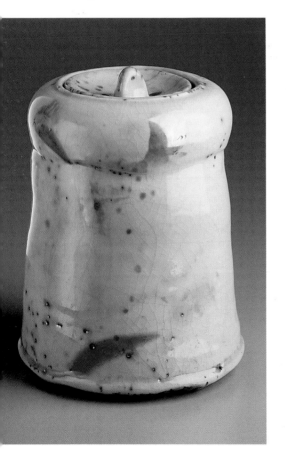

Andrew Mason (UK)

Following his early years spent in close proximity to the pottery industry in North Staffordshire, Andrew took a vocational Studio Pottery course. He subsequently taught part-time while setting up a pottery at Stone, Stafford-shire. He now works with his partner May Ling Beadsmoore at Darley Abbey in Derbyshire, where they have a showroom open to the public. Their individual work is very distinctive – May Ling makes soda-glazed domestic ware, while Andrew works in raku. Both, however, use colour as a major element in what they produce.

Andrew has a wide experience of different ceramic techniques, with the wheel serving as his main method of production. He makes finely composed shapes which need little or no finishing after they leave the wheel.

Andrew uses multi-coloured glazes on his thrown forms, giving the surfaces tremendous variety and depth. He writes: *Colour and pattern are built up in a fairly random fashion through spraying, trailing and brushing glazes, sometimes using latex resist which eventually reveals a black carbonised clay body, adding a further dimension to the aesthetic. A variety of visual imagery has acted as inspiration, from the spectacle of the aurora borealis (northern lights) to the deep, rich colours of autumn.*

Christine Fabre (F)

There is a harmony and a sense of history in Christine Fabre's work. It reaches for its sources into other cultures, especially (as I interpret her art) African, and in its surface treatment references other materials, including leather, fabrics and basketry. Indeed, it often incorporates different materials – twine, cord, weaving, wood, even a feather. Her work is clearly well-considered and lovingly made, and the various components of her finished pieces blend into something whole and mysterious.

Christine has exhibited widely in France for over 20 years. She writes: *As far as I am concerned, before taking any technical considerations into account, 'raku'* *is a state of mind. It consists of provoking 'accidents', more or less controlled, and each piece leads to an acceptance or rejection of that accident. Therefore raku is demanding, because it confronts us with ourselves without indulgence, it asks for rigour and fantasy, know-how and improvisation, softness and violence.*

Christine uses a white-firing stoneware clay, with added grog and talc. She biscuit fires to 1020°C (1868°F) in an electric kiln, and glaze fires to 1020°–1050°C (1868°–1922°F) in a ceramic fibre kiln.

Right Christine Fabre, box with cord addition, h. 30 cm (12 in.).
Below Christine Fabre, construction, length: 120 cm (47 in.).

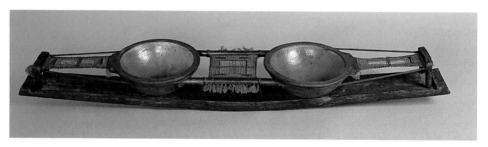

David Atamanchuk
(CAN/JAP)

David Atamanchuk's work has grown out of a long period of study, originally in his native Canada, and later in Japan. He attended art school in Vancouver, where he set up his own studio, producing functional pieces. In 1978 he travelled to Japan on a Japanese Ministry of Education Scholarship to study Oriental ceramics on the Aoyama University Master's course, and at the Idemitsu Museum of Art, Tokyo. During the first two years he studied their extensive shard collection – his special interest was overglazed enamels – and in his third and fourth years was allowed to handle everything in the collection, an experience which is the envy of many potters. In 1983 he was accepted into the Tokyo University of Arts and Music Ceramic Department, where he was the first to enter the Research Scholarship Programme. There he worked under Professors Yoshimichi Fujimoto and Koichi Tamura, both of whom were Tomimoto's and Kenichi's top students; during David's third and final year both were designated Living National

Treasures. In 1986 David set up his studio 93 miles (150 km) from Tokyo, where he has produced a variety of functional ware and has held a number of shows.

In the past, David has worked in white glazed porcelain, celadon, lustre ware, and Kobiki (slip-glazed ware). Today he makes raku, and saggar-fired stoneware using charcoal and copper, producing a range of colours on the unglazed surfaces of the pots. All his work is wheel-made, some pieces being distorted, others round or foliated, with added feet, lugs, and handles.

David's involvement with raku goes back to student days and he recounts that, at his first exhibition of raku pieces in Japan, potential customers found it difficult to accept raku being used for vases; in the Japanese mind, especially amongst the older generation, raku was reserved for the tea ceremony, its fragility unacceptable for anything else. For his second show David made adjustments to all aspects of the raku process (see Chapter Nine), in particular biscuit firing to 1150–1200°C (2102–2192°F). This, the highest temperature I know of in raku, produced a much

David Atamanchuk, vase.

David Atamanchuk, vessel form.

harder body which met with greater approval. Nevertheless, he finds that most of his customers are in their 30s and 40s.

He writes: *A number of years ago Raku Kichizaemon had a large show of newly-made raku pieces. The shapes were new, though all tea-related, and there were several new colours. The comments of the various people who viewed the pieces were, overall, not favourable, with many stating* *they had wanted to see more traditional work.* He also adds that to purchase a tea bowl from the current Raku Kichizaemon XVI would cost a small fortune!

Clays used:

• Shigaraki clay (heavily grogged)

David says that some Japanese potters make their own raku clay, others add grog to a standard body.

Berenice Kate Alcock (UK)

Berenice makes figurative work including heads, torsos, wall heads, and lifesize figures. She went straight from sixth form to the Ceramics course at the Central School of Art (London), where she was introduced to raku; during her final year she concentrated mainly on the raku process. After graduating she lived in Athens for some time; she now lives and works in the UK.

Berenice mainly coils her figures using a crank clay, though if she is to carry out a series she will make a plaster mould and subsequently alter each piece in some way. Work is biscuit fired to 1040°C (1904°F) in an electric kiln. She cites as her influences painters Rothko, Modigliani, Schiele and Lorca, sculptors Rodin and Jean Ipousteguy, and anything archaeological, especially from Greece and Egypt.

She writes: *The inner spirit of the people I meet in my life informs my work and gives me my direction. I am always searching for that depth of understanding I can share – sometimes painfully, and my works are symbols, an attempt to crystallise and hold my past and my present. This, I think, is the main reason I have been so drawn towards raku, for its nature is earthy and ancient and carries with it a sense of timelessness and includes the imperfections and flaws alongside the beauty that is within us.*

At its best raku should be wild and wonderful and given free reign; to demand control would be to deny its very spirit. Raku should be tackled head on, it is not for the fainthearted; to my mind a cautious or precious approach leads to disappointing results.

Clays used:
• Crank clay body

Berenice Kate Alcock, head from the 'Pageant Series'.

Berenice Kate Alcock, torso.

Robert Piepenburg (USA)

Robert has been making raku for over 30 years, and wrote the first edition of *Raku Pottery* in 1972; the latest edition was printed in 1998 (see Bibliography). He first came to raku when teaching with the limited facilities of two electric bisque kilns, and a lot of students, and so started a major raku programme.

Robert writes that raku 'provides the timeless surface for my kind of clay work', and that his forms are influenced by 'the material itself, (and) my inner need to manipulate form in a personally expressive/spiritual way'. This spiritual quest is very evident in his book; indeed I think most artists would acknowledge it as a major element in their own work, though their definitions may vary.

Robert makes wheel forms that are altered, and sculptural pieces from thick, stiff slabs of clay. He uses 'standard clay fabrication techniques; it's the quest for original forms that absorbs me.' Robert biscuit fires to cone 05 (1040°C/1904°F) in an electric kiln.

Robert sprays glazes that have a 'dry/copper metallic look'; the resulting finishes often give his pieces an ancient quality. Copper carbonate is an important glaze ingredient for him.

Clays used:

100	Hawthorn Bond Fireclay
50	Salt Lick Fireclay
60	Virginia Kyanite (35s mesh)

Robert Piepenburg, slab construction, 14 cm x 25 cm x 30 cm (5½ in. x 10 in. x 12 in.).

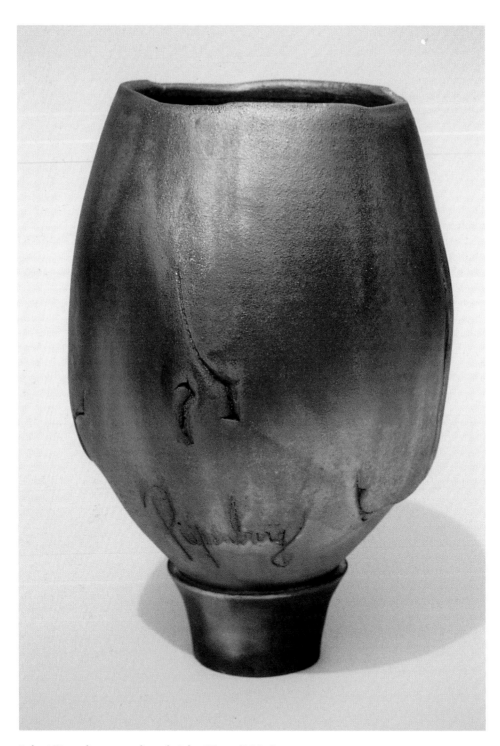

Robert Piepenburg, vase form, height: 28 cm (11 in.).

Peter Powning (CAN)

Originally from the United States, Peter Powning has lived and worked in New Brunswick, Canada, for over 30 years. He has had a distinguished career, and has exhibited widely internationally. He works 'in clay, bronze and glass – they all involve transformation by fire. That may be what drew me to them.' He will often combine these materials in the same piece. Of his involvement with raku he writes: 'I love the immediacy of the process, the sense of antiquity that can be achieved, and the textures possible.'

Peter produces a wide range of work, including copper-matt glazed pieces, vessel forms with carefully delineated patterns and images, sculptures reminiscent of ancient standing stones, wall panels, and reliquaries. He writes: *The work is meant to have the feel of an artefact. An emotional artefact made solid. A cultural artefact from some future/past, reconstructed or guessed at. Some parts original, some new, some assumed.*

Biscuit firing is to cone 04 (1065°C/1949°F). For the raku firing Peter uses up to five digitally-controlled electric kilns, and allows the pots to cool to 670°–705°C (1240°–1300°F) before placing them in the reduction containers.

Clays used:
• Ungrogged, whiteware-type throwing body
• Heavily grogged white stoneware body

'Reliquary Blue', height: 23 cm (9 in.).

Above Watering can, height: 46 cm (18 in.). *Below* Bowl, diameter: 46 cm (18 in.).

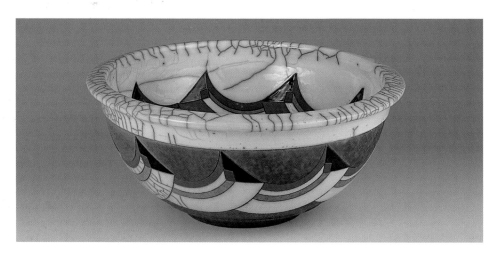

Anna Eilert (sw)

Anna Eilert makes large decorative relief
panels, often to commission, as well as
smaller sculptural pieces. She has been
greatly influenced in all her work by
her other major interest, archaeology,
and has taken part in excavations in
northern Sweden. Subsequent experiments with raku firing at art school,
which resulted in similar surface effects
to unearthed pieces of pottery, gave her
the artistic language she was seeking.
The soft earth colours she uses are
enlivened by careful use of copper.

Amongst her sculptures are tapering
pieces resembling ancient arrowheads.
These are sometimes wall-mounted,
sometimes supported on steel rods. She
uses mainly one glaze which gives
endless variations, depending on
thickness and firing differences.

Anna Eilert, arrowhead form, height: 60 cm
(24 in.).

Pat Armstrong (UK)

Pat works across a wide range of raku techniques, using glaze, copper matt, and resist slip techniques. Her work was initially influenced by ancient pots – she was attracted by the purity of line and the balance of profile. She likes small bases and flared rims, with gentle curves, and emphasises that her shapes have evolved unconsciously from influences seen in books, museums, and life. She feels the unpredictable finishes found in raku fit well with the clean lines of her chosen forms. She writes:

I have always been inspired by and in awe of fire – of pictures painted by flames and smoke, sparks against a night sky, fiery sunsets and not least by pictures of erupting volcanoes. More recently my inspiration has been fueled by pictures of far-off planets from the Hubble telescope. For a long time I sought to re-create these images and at last found I could at least start to achieve this by attempting to control the copper-fumed method of raku firing onto deceptively simple thrown shapes.

Pat later started experimenting with 'naked raku'. She enjoys the soft finish and loves picking off the glaze; in addition, it acts as a visual foil against the fumed copper pieces.

Clays used:
• Earthstone smooth-textured crank – for copper-fumed pots
• Earthstone smooth white clay – for small and medium glazed pots
• T-material for naked raku and large glazed pots

Left Anna Eilert, wall panel, height: 165 cm (65 in.).
Right Pat Armstrong, bottle, resist slip.

Peter Hayes (UK)

Peter went to Mosely School of Art and Craft at 13, but his introduction to clay only came when he moved on to Birmingham College of Art at 16. After a few years potting in Cornwall, Peter became director of a studio pottery in Lesotho, succeeding Geoffrey Whiting. This developed into the post of Crafts Advisor for the area – his transport allocation included three horses and a Land Rover. Later he was advisor for the development of ceramics under the auspices of the Commonwealth Fund for Technical Co-operation in Nepal, India, Japan and South Korea. On his return to the UK he was Craft Advisor for South-West Arts before setting up his own studio. His work has been exhibited internationally and is in many collections worldwide, both public and private.

Peter's work is diverse, but is characterised by having a timeless, weather-worn quality, often combined with the mysterious aura of ancient standing stones and artefacts. Textured slabs are first stretched by throwing them onto a board, where they pick up powdered clay; by repeating this process a multi-layered skin is built up. Pieces are then constructed from these slabs. By combining this textured clay with burnishing and polishing, Peter aims to achieve opposites of rough and smooth.

In addition, Peter introduces other minerals into the raku surface, such as iron and copper, sometimes molten copper. His pieces may then be submerged in the river beside his workshop, or in the sea, to allow time to work its own effect on the surfaces. Some sculptures have copper- or iron-saturated water flowing over them for months in the workshop.

Peter enjoys breaking the rules. He

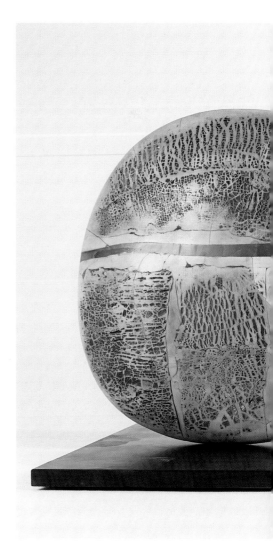

Peter Hayes, 'Three Pebbles with Blue Wave', mounted on Welsh slate, height: 122 cm x 61 cm (48 in. x 24 in.).

writes: *I find it joyful to work with many different clays, from bone china to crank. Each has its own character, its own limits, its own tolerance. I like doing raku firing with completely the 'wrong' clay, which I know will crack or explode in the kiln (especially when wet). But when all the pieces are stuck together and the surfaces*

are ground down it gives me a piece, a found object, with a pleasingly bruised and battered surface which has been carefully and lovingly honed down.

Peter re-assembles the broken clay using coloured epoxy resin; the resin gives the impression of molten minerals filling the interstices between fragments of stone. Hollow forms to be placed outdoors are filled with a type of polyester resin, and treated with sealant (available from hardware stores).

Recent work has included standing stones up to 3 m (10 ft) tall, placed in water. Peter concludes: *My main aim is not that my work should compete with nature but evolve within the environment.*

Safety note: It can be extremely dangerous to raku fire damp or wet clay. When water changes to steam it expands to approximately 22 times its original volume; water trapped inside a piece of work can result in a dramatic explosion.

107

Gail Bakutis (USA)

Shortly before midnight in October 1975, Gail fired her first raku pot in her studio in Hawaii. After removing it from the kiln, she carried the red-hot pot to the Pacific Ocean, where she quenched it in a tidal pool. In this dramatic setting Gail had begun her journey into raku.

Over the years Gail has produced a remarkable body of work, much of it involving temple forms and other architectural pieces, teapots which often relate to the temples, boxes and wall panels. There are two themes which run consistently throughout her work. Firstly, there is the influence of nature on the surfaces of her pieces. I was privileged to be given a private slide show by Gail during her residency at Rufford Ceramic Centre (UK), and saw amazing photographs of volcanic activity on Hawaii – eruptions, lava flows, and the 'frozen' crust of cooling lava; these amazing variations in surface features and colours are echoed in Gail's work. *The volcano inspires all my explorations in clay: its fire, its black, hard surface, its iridescence. It is a single,* powerful metaphor for the unity of destruction and creativity. *In addition, there is the effect of the raku fire, of which she writes: Over the years, looking carefully at my finished pieces, I can see that nature has stamped herself onto their exteriors: from the flame patterns on the matt surfaces to the infusion of smoke, to the random lustre and markings. The fire sears my work with an indefinable mystery I could never have designed or imparted alone. I have recognised and welcomed the fire as a sacred final element in the creation of my art.*

The other aspect of her work which Gail emphasises is the spiritual element, a constant in her writings, both about her work and about raku. She uses the studio as a sanctuary, 'my place of contemplation and refuge'. She refers to 'the sacred fire' and its transformative powers.

She writes: *Whether it is as the creator of a piece or as the viewer, art makes me feel closer, elevated in a non-verbal way beyond my private world to the Unknowable, to the Mystery of this life. As music defies definition or description in any language but its own, so art speaks to my soul. Timeless and speaking in all tongues, it can carry us to a*

Left Gail Bakutis, demonstrating. *Above* Gail Bakutis, 'Tea Fortress', height: 71 cm (28 in.).

place of beauty, not once but over and over again, to fill us with the wonder of creation, not just God's or nature's, but artists' as well.

Gail cannot envisage art – whether from the maker's or the viewer's perspective – as anything other than a spiritual experience. This, to me, is the heart of any artistic experience, though the definition of spiritual will vary with the individual, and may or may not include a religious element.

As Gail wants a pure white surface on which to develop her glazes, and because she does not know whether a piece will be fired as raku or as stoneware, she uses a porcelainous body which will fire to cone 10 (1290°C/ 2354°F) for her slab-built constructions. For her wall-pieces she uses paperclay, one third of which consists of recycled paper in pulp form, with the remainder being made up from her porcelain body and large quantities of various grogs and

kyanite. Sodium silicate and vinegar are added to the mix. The slabs of clay are prepared using Brent slab rollers.

Work is biscuit fired in both electric and gas kilns. For raku she has designed her own kilns, which are custom-made from galvanised metal and ceramic fibre blanket, and shaped like rectangular rings with no bottom. The kiln floor is a separate copper dish lined with fibre. By stacking the kiln rings on top of each other Gail is able to adjust the kiln to the size of the work being fired. As she usually works alone, she made the kiln sections so that she could lift them easily. In addition, she has a rolling reduction chamber which can be placed around work after the kiln sections have been removed, allowing her to reduce large pieces in situ.

Gail biscuit fires to cone 04 (1065°C/ 1949°F), and glazes at temperatures between 982°C (1800°F) and 1149°C (2100°F), 'depending on the glaze and the look I desire – there is no set rule'.

Gail Bakutis, 'Palanquin'.

John Mathieson (UK)

I started going to pottery evening classes whilst teaching in London, and was immediately hooked on clay. Within a few months I had read Bernard Leach's *A Potter's Book* and had begun Saturday classes at the Sir John Cass College in Whitechapel. Less than a year after first using clay I was teaching ceramics and art at secondary level – daunting at first, but I was on a fast learning curve and enthralled by what I was doing. (I still am.) Later I was given secondment to take a degree (one year part-time, one year full-time) and even sold some of my work to the external examiners! A few years ago I left teaching, though I still teach evening classes. I reckon I did something upward of 8,000 firings during my time in school.

My work has mainly been thrown, though I have made a number of slab pieces. I've never made coil pots – too time-consuming for my temperament – but I love the way they feel. I work on a slow Leach kickwheel using soft clay, usually equal parts of T-material and porcelain. (I sometimes use DSS from Doble's, an excellent stoneware clay with a small iron content which gives a pink tinge to the glaze). Influenced by the Leach 'tradition' I began by making functional pots, but have increasingly moved away from that to individual pieces which may or may not be functionally related. I am not happy with the word 'tradition' and never sought to work within one. (The term seems confining, although I have read an excellent essay – see Bibliography – by Mike Dodd on tradition as a living and evolving force.) Rather, I make what I want to make, hopefully with the sources of my inspiration having been absorbed and forgotten, to allow their influence to develop into something personal. I have a preoccupation with certain forms, especially bowls and

Author, tea bowl on stand, diameter: 11 cm (4½ in.). *Photograph by the author.*

Author, 'Vases for a Single Memory', height (tallest): 25 cm (10 in.) *Photograph by author.*

bottles. And as I work in reduced stoneware as well as raku, both the overlaps and the differences can be intriguing.

I find it difficult to discuss my completed work, and all but impossible to evaluate it. There is a very real sense in which, when a piece has been finished, it has left me. I am never satisfied with my work, but once in a while something comes from the kiln which is as both my heart and my head feel it, when the kiln god, my efforts, the form and the glaze all seem to me to

have combined reasonably well in a piece, and I think this is as it should be.

My work is biscuit fired in a 7 cu. ft (0.2 m³) propane kiln to 980°C (1796°F), and glaze-fired to 900°C (1650°F) in a fibre-lined oil drum, again using propane. I reduce in sawdust or fine woodshavings.

Clays used:
• Potclays White St.Thomas with 10 – 20% grog
• Equal parts of T-material and Potclays HF Porcelain
• DSS from Doble's
• Recently experimenting with clays from Scarva

John Wheeldon (UK)

In addition to making, John teaches, runs the West End Gallery in Wirksworth, Derbyshire, and is a Council Member of the Craft Potters Association of Great Britain. He is well known for his copper-matt glazed pieces, mainly wheel-made with hand-formed additions for lids, handles, and feet.

John biscuit fires in an electric kiln quite quickly to 950°C (1742°F), raising the kiln 80°C (176°F) an hour to 160°C (320°F), then 160°C (320°F) to temperature. He often applies decorative lines and marks using latex in a manner very akin to slip-trailing. Many of his forms have a thick sieved body slip

John Wheeldon, lidded jar, copper-matt glaze.

applied in a similar way when leatherhard. When dry, the pots are dipped in the copper-matt glaze, and the latex subsequently removed. During the firing the exposed body becomes black and grey, which contrasts with the often brilliantly coloured glaze. The rim and top section of John's pieces are usually left unglazed, partly as a further visual play, and partly for practical reasons, as the pots are inverted for reduction.

Clays used:

• ST material from Commercial Clays

John Wheeldon, vase.

Chapter Eleven
Slip and Glaze Recipes

GLAZE RECIPES
David Roberts (UK)

Crackle White 1

Calcium borate frit	40
Borax frit	
(Potterycrafts 2955)	40
China clay	15
Tin oxide	5

Open crazing.

Crackle White 2

High alkali frit	80
China clay	15
Tin oxide	5

Fine crazing.

Transparent glaze 1

Soft borax frit	85
China clay	15

An open crazing.
Often used with added oxides and stains as cover for pattern work.

Transparent glaze 2

High alkali frit	85
China clay	15

Finer crazing.

Dry copper glaze

Borax frit	60
Powdered St.Thomas clay	30
Copper oxide	5
Red iron oxide	5

10 – 15 minutes heavy reduction in the kiln increases lustre.

Tim Andrews (UK)

Main glaze

High alkaline frit	40
China clay	10
Quartz	10

Copper-matt

Copper oxide	80
Frit	20

'Plus a little iron oxide sometimes'.

David Jones (UK)

When I asked David for his glaze firing temperature, his reply was: *I'm afraid there is no answer. When the pots are cooked I take them out of the kiln! In 20 years I have never put a thermocouple into my kiln. It is one of the great pleasures of raku not to need to worry about precision.*

Base glaze

High alkali frit	85
China clay	15
Bentonite	5

Oxide additions

Cobalt oxide	2 (blue)
Copper carbonate	1 (turquoise)
Tin oxide	7 (white)
Gold chloride	¼

Silver/gold/yellow

High alkali frit	50
Lithium carbonate	35
China clay	10
Bentonite	5
Silver nitrate	1.5

Rob Sollis (UK)

As with many other raku potters, Rob has never fired with a pyrometer and does not know the maturing tempera-ture of his glazes. To achieve a denser surface, he fires his blackware some 15°C (59°F) higher by eye than his glazed pieces.

Base glaze

Standard borax frit	8 5
Grolleg china clay	1 5

Additions of copper carbonate
up to 2 ½ % – (pale blue)
up to 10% – (deep green)
10% and reduce *inside* the kiln for
    copper reds and lustres.

John Mathieson (UK)

For what I refer to as 'splash lines' over the base glaze (borax frit and china clay), I mix oxides and borax frit very approximately by volume (measuring with a spoon) in plastic honey jars – it is never the same twice. The mixtures are sieved only to prevent the slip-trailers becoming blocked.

5–15% copper carbonate in a borax frit gives a range of greens (copper with reduction in the kiln)

1–5% cobalt oxide or carbonate gives blues

1–10% iron oxide gives pale yellows to dark browns

1–5% chrome oxide gives a strong green with limited crackle

Andrew Mason (UK)

Base glaze

Frit	82
(varying percentages of standard alkaline and borax frit)	
China clay	8
Ball clay	8
Bentonite	2

Fired to 1080°C (1976°F).

Andrew writes: *A high percentage of metal oxides and/or glaze stains are added to the base glaze and applied thinly, eg. copper oxide 6%. Alkaline is good for copper and cobalt, borax for iron and manganese.*

John Wheeldon (UK)

Copper-matt glaze

Copper oxide	90
Alkaline frit	10

Fired to 1000°C (1832°F).

Pat Armstrong (UK)

Copper-matt glaze

Copper oxide	90
High alkaline frit	10
Bentonite	2

Plus some wallpaper paste
Fired to 900°–950°C (1652°–1742°F).

Pat also uses high alkali raku glazes to which she adds:
Copper oxide plus chrome oxide (green)
Copper oxide plus tin oxide (turquoise)
Copper oxide plus cobalt oxide (blue)

Berenice Kate Alcock (UK)

Potclays 2202 general purpose leadless transparent glaze, fired to 1020°C (1868°F).

Tony and Barbara White (UK)

Low temperature earthenware brush-on glazes.

Lynda Harris (NZ)

Apple crackle

Gerstley borate	80
Feldspar	20

Copper lustre

Gerstley borate	80
Feldspar	20
Copper carbonate	20
Iron oxide	5

Fired to 1000°C (1832°F).
Needs heavy reduction to produce metallic copper.

Ellen Rijsdorp (NL)

Transparent glaze

Calcium borate	100
Lead bisilicate	30
Kaolin	50

Fired to 980°C (1796°F).

Jannie van der Wel (NL)

Turquoise glaze

Alkali frit (1510)	63.5
Alkali borosilicate frit	24
Tin oxide	4
Copper carbonate	4.5
Bentonite	4

Fired to around 925°C (1697°F).

Copper-matt glaze

Copper carbonate	80
Alkali frit (1510)	10
Powdered clay	10

Fired to 975°–1000°C (1787°–1832°F).

Nesrin During (NL)

Base glaze

Alkali borate frit	70
Kaolin	30

Fired to 900°–950°C (1652°–1742°F).

Oxide additions

1–3% iron oxide (pink to pomegranate reds in oxidation, and greys in reduction).
2–3% copper carbonate (Granny Smith apple green in oxidation to red in reduction).

Anna Eilert (SW)

Main glaze

Frit 3770	48
Lithium carbonate	15
Quartz	37
Tin oxide	2
Copper oxide	2

'This is my main glaze. The variations are never ending depending on thickness, oxidation or reduction.'

Gertrud Båge (SW)

Slips and oxide mixtures for use on biscuit ware, often without a glaze.

'Linda'

Gerstley borate	10
Nepheline syenite	10
Copper carbonate	10

Dark nut brown to black if applied thinly without a glaze. Gives a beautiful chestnut brown if applied thickly and reduced standing free in flames. Can be used as copper painting over glaze.

Iron with flux

Gerstley borate	10
Nepheline syenite	10
Iron oxide	10

Gives brown-red, depending on glaze; without a glaze gives brown-black, depending on reduction. Can be used as iron painting over glaze.

Reddish-brown

Gerstley borate	30
China clay	20
Quartz	10
Iron oxide	4

Gives reddish brown, depending on glaze; light brown to black without a glaze. Use thinly under a glaze.

Oxide mixtures

Use thinly over the glaze.

Moss green

Ochre	3
Copper oxide	1
Alkaline borax frit	5

Bluish green

Tin oxide	3
Copper oxide	2.5
Alkaline borax frit	5

Blue

Cobalt oxide	1
Copper oxide	1
Alkaline borax frit	5

Bluish violet

Manganese dioxide	5
Cobalt oxide	1
Iron oxide	3
Alkaline borax frit	5

Glazes

R48 glaze

Frit 3770	48
Lithium carbonate	15
Quartz	37

Fired to 1000°C (1832°F).

Oxide additions to R48 glaze

Tin oxide 5% (white)

Copper oxide 2% plus tin oxide 2% (turquoise)

Copper oxide 2% plus tin oxide 4% plus and cobalt oxide 1% (blue)

Cobalt oxide 1.5% plus copper oxide 1.5% plus iron oxide 5% plus black stain 3% (black)

Chrome oxide 2% plus tin oxide 5% (chrome green)

Grey stain 5% plus tin oxide 3% (grey)

Cobalt oxide 1% plus tin oxide 4% plus 0.3% coarse copper oxide (bluish violet with copper spots)

Orange stain 6% plus 0.3% coarse copper oxide (yellow-reddish-green)

J19 glaze

Frit J (or frit F)	68
Quartz	18
Lithium carbonate	6
Zinc oxide	8

Fired to 1000°C (1832°F).

Oxide additions to J19 glaze

Tin oxide 5% (white)

Cobalt oxide 2% plus copper oxide 4% plus tin oxide 4% (blue)

Iron oxide 4% (yellow)

Copper oxide 2–3% plus iron oxide 4% (green)

Copper oxide 1% plus iron oxide 4% (olive green)

Iron oxide 12 – 17% (brown)

Gertrud and Lena add wallpaper paste (cellulose glue) to the glazes in order to give a thick coating and make glazing with a brush easier. Gertrud points out that mixing leftovers of glaze can result in some beautiful colours. They also use double glazing, variations of glaze thickness, and different re-glazing and refiring.

Note: Gertrud has been told by her suppliers that Ferro are no longer making Frit 3770, and have suggested she replaces it with Blythe Frit 2691.

Pietro Maddalena (I)

Crackle glaze
Alkaline frit	40
Borax frit	40
China clay	12
Quartz	5

Tim writes: 'This will take the addition of colours well – for instance, 5 parts tin oxide for white, 5 parts copper oxide for green.'

Copper-matt
Alkaline frit	20
Ball clay	30
Copper oxide	40
Iron oxide	5
Molybdenum oxide	2
Tin oxide	2

Peter Powning (CAN)

Peter uses a range of glazes formulated for him by a glaze chemist, plus 'a range of time-honoured recipes from books, friends, and magazine articles'.

David Atamanchuk (CAN/JAP)

Clear glaze
Feldspar	33.5
Colemanite	41.5
Barium carbonate	14
Silica	11

Applied quite thickly and fired to 1000°C (1832°F).

Kristin Doner (USA)

Unearthed glaze
Lithium carbonate ⎤
Borax ⎥
Feldspar ⎬ (various quantities)
Bentonite ⎥
Colourant ⎦

Kristin invested a great deal of time researching this glaze and so is understandably unwilling to disclose the exact amounts of each material in the recipe. However, some educated experimentation with the ingredients should lead to a glaze unique to yourself.

Bob Smith (USA)

White crackle
Gerstley borate	80
Nepheline syenite	20
Kaolin	5
Zircopax (opacifier)	4

Glossy copper
Gerstley borate	52
Nepheline syenite	28
Soda feldspar	15
Kaolin	5
Copper carbonate	4

Both glazes are fired to cone 06 or higher (1000°C/1832°F) in an electric kiln, then given a further raku firing.

Robert Piepenburg (USA)

'Piepenburg Patina'
Gerstley borate	4
Bone ash	3
Nepheline syenite	2
Copper carbonate	1

'Alligator'
Gerstley borate	4
Bone ash	2
Nepheline syenite	1

Copper carbonate 1
Both glazes fired to 1024°–1038°C (1875°–1900°F), and applied by spraying.

Rick Foris (USA)

White crackle
Gerstley borate 80
Feldspar 20
For a turquoise variation add:
Copper carbonate 4
Cobalt carbonate ½
Fired to cones 08–06 (950°–1000°C/1742°–1832°F).

Rick Hirsch (USA)

Rick's WOW white
Gerstley borate 40
Frit 3110 40
Nepheline syenite 20
EPK 8

Rick's clear glaze
Frit 3110 60
Frit 3124 20
Nepheline syenite 20
Gerstley borate 20
EPK 8
Add 10% tin oxide for white.
Use over coloured slips or terra sigillatas.
(Note: EPK is China clay)

SLIPS, RESIST SLIPS AND RESIST GLAZES

David Roberts (UK)

Resist slip
China clay 3
Flint 2
Applied to the biscuit-fired pot.

Resist glaze
Alkali frit 45
Soft borax frit 45
China clay 10
Applied over the resist slip.

Black and white linear patterns
Body clay sieved through 200s mesh with gum arabic and painted on the biscuit-fired surface. This is removed after the firing, leaving lightly smoked areas which contrast with the darker, unprotected sections.

Tim Andrews (UK)

Slips
Tim writes: *'Slips can be just the clay body, sieved and with coloured body stains added. The quantity of stain depends on my whim at the time'.* He has been experimenting with grinding slips and stains down to a very small particle size (to give the appearance of terra sigillata) in a ball mill. *'Even 40 hours in a ball mill will only take a stain down to around 5 microns and I am looking for 1–2 microns.'*

Tim uses terra sigillata made in the usual way and applied onto leatherhard or dry pieces.

Resist slip
Equal parts china clay and quartz, with 5–10% aluminium hydroxide to aid adhesion.

Susan Luker (UK)

Susan uses a resist slip composed of 3 parts china clay and 2 parts flint, which she pours over the pot.

Resist glaze
Borax frit 46
High alkali frit 46
China clay 8
Applied by pouring. Will work well as a normal glaze.

Ellen Rijsdorp (NL)

Naked raku glaze
Kali feldspar	6
Bentonite	4
Calcium carbonate	16.2
Flint	3.9
Alkaline borax frit	53.5
Alkali frit	16.4

Applied over a thin slip and fired to 800°C (1472°F).

Kristin Doner (USA)

Resist slip
Lincoln 60 fireclay	40
No.6 tile clay	30
Fine or medium grog	20
Custer feldpar	10

Resist glaze
Ferro frit 3110	60
Gerstley borate	40

Rick Hirsch (USA)

Red terra sigillata
Red Art clay	50
Red iron oxide	50

Ball mill for 24 hours.

White terra sigillata
Ball clay	100

Ball mill for 24 hours.
Add ceramic stains for other colours.

Chapter Twelve
Conclusion

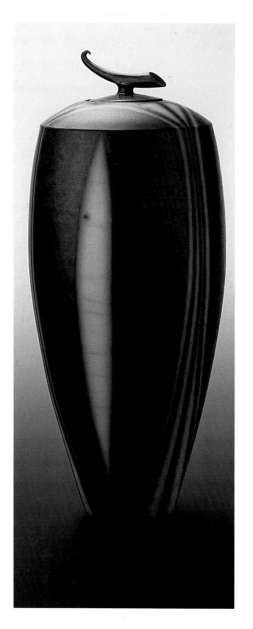

It is very important to remember that the whole learning process should be enjoyable – discovering different techniques, exploring ideas, finding out what is right for you, what to disregard, the how-to and the why. Yes, it is difficult at first. When Buddy Guy and Eric Clapton first picked up a guitar they sounded awful. But however proficient you become, the learning never stops, there are always new ideas to consider, and more questions to ask.

I believe we all have artistic abilities, and the realisation of these in clay or paint or music is the product of that innate sensibility. It is informed by what we see and experience, by what we consider, by what we absorb and by what we reject. Our individual journeys should be reflected in our preferred art form, in what we as potters choose to make. Raku is a wonderful medium for facilitating this.

Tim Andrews – tall lidded 'curling' pot, height: 46 cm (18 in.).

Suppliers

UK

Bath Potters Supplies
Unit 18, Fourth Avenue, Westfield
Trading Estate, Radstock, Bath BA3 4XE
Tel: 01761 411077
Website: www.bathpotters.demon.co.uk

Briar Wheels & Supplies Ltd
Whitsbury Road, Fordingbridge, Hants
SP6 1NQ
Tel: 01425 652991
www. briarwheels.co.uk

Commercial Clay Ltd
Sandbach Road, Cobridge, Stoke-on-
Trent ST6 2DR
Tel: 01782 274448

Corby Kilns Ltd
Priors Court, Priors Haw Road, Weldon,
Corby NN17 5JG
Tel: 01536 269229
Website: www.corbykilns.co.uk
*Repairs and maintenance of electric kilns,
plus reconditioned equipment*

CTM Supplies
9 Spruce Close, Exeter EX4 9JU
Tel: 01395 233077
Website: www.ctmsupplies.co.uk
For oxides, raw materials, tools

Craftline
Cairneycroft, 133 Draycott Old Road,
Forsbrook, Stoke-on-Trent ST11 9AJ
Tel: 01782 393222

W.J. Doble Pottery Clays
Newdowns Sand and Clay Pits,
St. Agnes, Cornwall TR5 0ST
Tel: 01872 552979

Metrosales
Unit 3, 46 Mill Place, Kingston-upon-
Thames, Surrey KT1 2RL
Tel: 020 8546 1108
e-mail: sales@metrosales.co.uk
*Pottery equipment and materials, plus a
good leaflet on Ian Gregory's flat-pack kiln*

Northern Kilns
Pilling Pottery, School Lane, Pilling,
Nr. Garstang, Lancashire PR3 6HB
Tel: 01253 790307
Website: www.northernkilns.com
Supply kilns and will custom build

Potclays Ltd
Brickkiln Lane, Etruria,
Stoke-on-Trent ST4 7BP
Tel: 01782 219816
Website: www.potclays.co.uk

The Potters Connection Ltd
Chadwick Street, Longton, Stoke-on-
Trent ST3 1PJ
Tel: 01782 598729
Website: www.pottersconnection.com

Potterycrafts Limited
Campbell Road, Stoke-on-Trent ST4 4ET
Tel: 01782 745000
Website: www.potterycrafts.co.uk

Scarva Pottery Supplies
Unit 20, Scarva Road Industrial Estate,
Banbridge, Co. Down BT32 3QD
Tel: 01820 669699
Website: www.scarvapottery.com

Spencroft Ceramics
Spencroft Road, Holditch Industrial
Estate, Newcastle, Staffordshire ST5 9JB
Tel: 01782 627004
For clays

Top Pot Supplies
Celadon House, 8 Plough Lane,
Newport, Shropshire TF10 8BS
Tel: 01952 813203

Valentine Clays
The Sliphouse, 18–20 Chell Street,
Hanley, Stoke-on-Trent ST1 6BA
Tel: 01782 271200

North America

American Art Clay Co. Inc.
4717 W.16th Street, Indianapolis,
IN 46222
Tel: 317 244 6871
Website: www.amaco.com
(Products include Brent slab rollers.)

Atlantic Pottery Supplies
15 Canal Street, Dartmouth B2Y 2W19,
Nova Scotia
Tel: (902) 466 6947

Axner pottery Supplies
P.O. Box 621484, Oviedo, FL 32765
Tel: 800 843 7057
Website: www.axner.com

Claymaker
1240 North 13th Street, San Jose,
CA 95112
Tel: (408) 295 3352
Website: www.claymaker.com

Clay People
112 Ohio Avenue, Unit 1, Richmond,
CA 94804
Tel: (510) 236 1492

Doug Gates
P.O. Box 103, Saluda, NC 28773
Tel: (828) 749 1181
Leach treadle wheels

East Bay Clay
200 South First Street, Richmond,
CA 94804
Tel: (510) 233 1800

Hampshire Woodworking
116 Pleasant Street, Easthampton,
MA 01027
Tel: (413) 527 8526
Leach treadle wheels

Laguna Clay Company
1440 Lomitas Avenue, City of Industry,
CA 91746
Tel: 800 452 4862
Website: www.lagunaclay.com

Leslie Ceramics Supply Company
1212 San Pablo Avenue, Berkeley,
CA 94706
Tel: (510) 524 7363

Mile Hi Ceramics
77 Lipan Street, Denver, CO 80223
Tel: (303) 825 4570
Website: www.MileHiCeramics.com

Paoli Clay Company
6879 Paoli Road, Paoli, WI 53508
Tel: (608) 845 7000

Plainsman Clays Limited
Box 1266, 702 Wood Street, Medicine
Hat, Alberta T1A 7M9
Tel: (403) 527 8535
Website: www.plainsmanclays.com